DEVIL'S PLAYGROUND

Devil's Playground

God's country has blood on its hands

Nova West

Los Angeles, California

Devil's Playground
Copyright © 2020 Nova West

All rights reserved. No part of this book may be reproduced by any means without the written permission of the publisher, except for short passages used in critical reviews.

All images used in this book are copyright © 2020 Nova West or are in the public domain.

Published By:
Genius Book Publishing
31858 Castaic Road #154
Castaic, CA 91384
GeniusBookPublishing.com

ISBN: 978-1-947521-19-3

200131

Dedication

I dedicate this book to Vonda Smith, and to all the wrongly convicted victims of the world. May their experience with injustice teach us all a lesson and may God be with them and their loved ones. In turn, this is a book for Jessie Morrison and her unborn baby as well. May the devil's playgrounds of America burn to the ground and the people become phoenixes, rising from the ashes to start anew.

Preface

Devil's Playground is the result of my mom's and my investigation into a wrongful conviction but is by no means the finale. What started as an amateur rescue attempt morphed into an investigation to find a killer, which opened the flood gates of wickedness. We found ourselves engulfed by a small town's corruption, finding more questions than answers. This story traverses our journey and the many paths we walked, and the rabbit holes we fell into in our quest for answers and justice.

I would like to recognize my mom for her invaluable work on this case and for the hundreds of hours, if not over a thousand, spent sleuthing and researching. This book would not exist without her efforts and I am forever grateful for all her help and support. Special thanks to my publisher, Steven Booth and his wife, Leya, for believing in me and for their contagious enthusiasm. Last, but not least, I want to thank my husband and children for their support and understanding during my time spent working on the case and the creation of this story. They consumed many frozen meals and survived a wife and mother on the edge for quite some time.

Oh my, I almost forgot someone! I offer my gratitude to my rival blogger, Hailey. Her contempt for me and my blog about the case, along with her backhanded compliment of my storytelling ability, encouraged me to reach for the stars and write this book.

Introduction

In the beautiful Appalachian region, that can only be described as God's country, there is a wickedness. Hiding beneath the landscape's beauty is a darkness that once seen can never be unseen. The murder of a young pregnant mother, followed by the arrest and conviction of an unexpected suspect, prompted a mother and daughter to search for the truth.

The pair's initial quest, seeking justice for the wrongly convicted suspect, blossomed into an amateur investigation of the murder case. The gumshoe heroines' exploration of the case's details and omitted particulars revealed a much broader picture of the devil's playground they now faced.

Mother and daughter found themselves championing freedom and justice, investigating a murder and questioning the truth. Who killed Jessie? Who framed Vonda? Why did it appear the county had so many secrets and why did it feel as though everyone had blood on their hands but the suspect?

You are invited to join the quest and are hereby inaugurated a sleuth. Follow the trail, search for clues and question everything. A great mystery requires solving, can you help?

Chapter One

I'm not a professional investigator and I was not an author. I'm an ordinary person who's found herself in an extraordinary situation. I have a story to share and I'll try my best to tell it. Some names have been changed to protect private citizens' identities.

Lights a cigarette

Let's start at the beginning, shall we? Jessie was a 21-year-old mother of two young boys and was sixteen weeks pregnant with her third child when she was brutally murdered on Friday evening, August 12th, 2016 in Greene County, Tennessee. Two days after her death, I was in labor and delivery welcoming my second child into the world, so my account and recollection of the next year and a half following the murder is a bit fuzzy.

I can recall being told about the murder sometime after I had given birth, but I didn't know the victim, was unaware of the circumstances and had only met Vonda once or twice before, so my level of interest was minimal at best. Looking back, maybe I should have been more interested.

Fast forward roughly two months and still in my baby haze, I heard about Vonda disappearing one night in October 2016 and then being found the next morning in a ditch, beaten the hell up, but alive. Fast forward again to March 2017 and Vonda is ultimately arrested for Jessie's murder. I remained in my baby haze and quiet life until Vonda's trial in May 2018.... That's when everything changed.

Each spring my family and I take a road trip out West and 2018's trip had us at my grandma's house in Arizona the week of the trial, which only lasted from May 22nd through the 25th. The final day of the trial was on the Friday of Memorial Day weekend. Astonishingly, deliberation only took six short hours and then... "guilty."

Our family's mood before and during the trial was hopeful because we honestly believed there was no way Vonda would be convicted. Surely the jury would see that this woman clearly did not commit this crime. The verdict came as a complete shock. Once we found out about the verdict, I instinctively knew it was up to me to help. Our family was stunned and didn't know what to do and, frankly, neither did I. But I didn't let that stop me.

My mom had met us in Arizona, and was there at my grandma's visiting from Georgia. We all sat at the patio table, beers in one hand and our phones in the other. I called a family member back home in Tennessee to get the rundown about the verdict and the trial. I had grabbed a modest stack of Post-It notes and a pen and began scribbling down all the information I could get my hands on. In hindsight, my little square Post-It notes never stood a chance. Just hours into the case, they were all stuck—stacked together in complete disarray. It was a chaotic scene in those first couple of hours; each of us on our phone either making calls, texting, emailing or researching, the beer bottles and cans piling up alongside our notes. Back then, in those first hours... I almost can't recall what we accomplished exactly, but that was the beginning of this story.

It had crossed my mind more than once that I should be patient and wait until we got home to start on this case because I had enough sense even then to realize I ought to buy a burner phone for this sort of operation, but I'm an impatient idiot and disregarded my intuition.

Once we were home, my quiet life was no more. My mom had returned to her home as well and that's when we joined forces. Initially, we were armed with just enough information, a few names and Facebook. Yeah, that's how our investigation got off the ground… fucking Facebook.

Prior to the trial and the crusade that we launched afterward, my mom had joined Reddit for news and for shits and giggles. She would periodically tell me about funny ha-ha's she had read or current affairs that were trending. One day during the summer of 2018, she suggested I join and post about this case. We were in need of some publicity, so I created an account and started typing. It felt good to finally have an outlet to share what I was going through with the case. I couldn't have known at the time, but my Reddit thread would eventually be viewed over 12,000 times during the course of that summer.

It was in June, just a couple of weeks following the trial, that we (my mom and I) got our first big break immediately followed by a second. I couldn't tell you the exact date, but I remember the day vividly. I was at Vonda's sister-in-law's house visiting with Pam and her husband, Dale. Vonda's husband Don (Pam's brother) was also there visiting.

A day or two prior to my visit, my mom had found a retired forensic expert by the name of David, who I reached out to via e-mail. David called me. Our conversation flowed easily, and I gave him additional details about the case and answered his questions. By the end of the conversation, he was not only willing to help, but he said he'd work pro-bono. Score!

Just as I had finished excitedly chirping my way through the great news about David to the family, I got another phone call. This one was from Mike, a retired FBI agent I had e-mailed a few weeks earlier. Keep in mind… when I first started working on this murder case/wrongful conviction, I had no idea what I was doing, so I ran in every direction possible. One included reaching out to nearly one hundred retired FBI agents I had found listed on a website. Why did we need someone of such caliber? Well, we'll get to that a little later. The point is, Mike was calling.

Mike and I talked for some time and our personalities seemed to sync right off the bat. He was a "Yankee" and I desperately needed an outsider like that to help. By the end of that conversation, he was very interested in the case, willing to help. And he also offered to work pro-bono. Double score! These two phone calls left me bursting with hope and I felt such relief that we finally had some real help.

There we were... only one month after the trial and an ordinary mom and daughter team had worked so hard and so fast that we had developed a list of potential suspects, a possible motive or two, we had a retired forensic expert and a retired FBI agent on board and a swelling Reddit thread that a huge chunk of small-town Greeneville was talking about. It appeared our luck was on the rise, but that soon changed. A sobering bit of information found its way to me and that would only be the start of more to come.

I got a phone call from a family friend one day telling me that the D.A was looking for the writer of my Reddit thread. For those of you that might not know, D.A stands for "district attorney," which is the prosecutor/prosecution team. Apparently, there was a girl who worked for an attorney in town and the D.A assumed that this girl was the writer. I was told that this girl showed up to work one morning and her boss (the attorney) called her into his office. He told her to stop writing nonsense online. Confused, the girl asked him what the hell he was talking about. He told her he had just gotten off the phone with the D.A, who had called to warn him that his employee needed to keep her mouth shut. When her boss explained to her that it was about the Reddit thread on Vonda Smith's case, the girl laughed in his face and told him that she wasn't the writer, but that he should read it because it was good.

When I heard this story, I had a couple different emotions about it. My ego felt a bit boosted, but the reality was that the

D.A was looking for me over this and that scared me. It was in that moment that I first really realized the seriousness of the case and my suspicions were confirmed... this was big.

As if being hunted wasn't bad enough, our rescuers, David and Mike, were being cockblocked by Vonda's own attorney. I didn't have contact with Vonda or "Steven," her attorney, so I had to communicate with the only liaison, Vonda's youngest son, Curtis. He was the one who had hired Steven, and was the family member in contact with him. David and Mike had been waiting in the wings for Steven to call them, but he wasn't calling and my patience was wearing thin.

The thing is, I hate "middlemen." I hate the middleman even more if he doesn't do his job. I had facilitated all of this... yet Steven wasn't jumping on this once-in-a-lifetime opportunity that we desperately needed, and I became suspicious as to why. I decided to bypass our liaison, Curtis, and called Steven's office myself. The voicemail I left was professional, polite and to the point. I never did hear from Steven, but I sure heard from Curtis. He sent me a mildly nasty text message explaining that he was in charge and that no one was to contact Steven other than him. Well, well, well... I hadn't seen that coming. That was the moment I began to question what was really going on.

July 4th, 2018 came and went. Just a day or two after, I got a call from Vonda's sister-in-law, Pam. She told me that she had just gotten off the phone with Curtis. He had told her that Steven finally called David. Pam went on to relay that Steven told Curtis that during his phone conversation with David, the retired forensic expert said he was no longer willing to help because of something I had written on Reddit.

I called David. I asked him politely but directly what his conversation was with Vonda's attorney. He gave me an entirely different story, which I was inclined to believe over Steven's version. My Reddit thread was never mentioned during their conversation and, contrary to what Steven told Curtis, David was still very much willing to help. Why did Vonda's own attorney lie? What the hell was going on?

Shortly after the Steven/David debacle, I received an e-mail from Mike. He told me that Steven had finally contacted him too, but to my surprise… Steven had agreed to bring Mike on board. To get the ball rolling, Steven faxed Mike a confidentiality agreement to sign. This type of contract is standard in a criminal case and it is binding. The second Steven received the contract with Mike's signature on it, it prevented Mike from discussing the case with anyone other than Steven. We didn't realize it at the time, but what Steven had done was both brilliant and damning. That little shit never had any intention of working with Mike. He essentially sequestered him with the agreement, rendering Mike legally incapable of assisting anyone with this case other than Vonda's attorney. Well played, Steven, well played.

Steven's manipulative power move and choice to not accept the help from these two professionals was a flaming red flag. Was Steven sabotaging his own case? Why would he do that? Had he been threatened? Had he been bought off? Was he in someone's pocket? If Steven was a puppet, who was holding the strings?

My mom and I felt like we had hit a brick wall. Vonda's hearing for an appeal was scheduled for August 4th, 2018, but the day never came. We were told the reason for it being rescheduled was due to the trial transcripts not being ready yet… another brick wall. After all that had happened in the weeks between July 4th and August 4th, we felt defeated. I made the executive decision to take my first break from the case. I needed to spend quality time with my two kids and recharge. I halted my posting on Reddit and left my followers and readers hanging. What I hadn't known at the time was that just as I was entering my hiatus, a rival blogger was emerging.

Two weeks into my hiatus, my mom started texting again about the case. I should have known she wasn't going to just drop it and walk away as easily as I thought I had. She sucked me right back into it by dangling new potential leads in front of me. I took the bait, of course. I removed my proverbial detective hat from its hook and placed it on my head again. I was back.

I revisited Reddit and realized it was no longer the best platform for me to continue writing about the case. The thread had become jumbled with all my posts and was difficult to follow. It had morphed into a blog and that transformation led me to Tumblr.

Once I had copied and pasted every post from Reddit over to Tumblr, I continued to post about the case and, more to the point, I continued to illustrate my train of thought and the perspectives I held. My entire blog, from the beginning, is written gonzo style with a heavy anecdotal layer. Numerous simple minds could not wrap their brains around my writing and more than a handful of those simple minds took their ignorance and attacked me with it.

There was one such soul who stood out among the rest and that person positioned herself as my rival. Hailey had started a blog of her own about the case in mid-August 2018 and was out for blood… my blood.

The content in one of her earliest posts included attacking me in the form of shaming and scrutinizing my blog. She called me a liar and asserted I was a lunatic. Hailey did, however, compliment my storytelling ability, which she later attributed to the success of the "fiction" I was pumping out about the case. It was evident she didn't understand my intentions, nor could she comprehend the position I had put myself in.

As time went on and as I continued to blog, and as Hailey continued to as well, I learned that she had been a follower of mine in my early days of Reddit. I had actually heard her name prior to her starting her blog. Over the summer she had messaged a couple of Vonda's relatives, desperate to get information about the case. From what I remember, Hailey was both rude and arrogant in her approach and because of that each and every family member either refused her requests or ignored them completely.

It wasn't until early in 2019 that I learned Hailey had written to Vonda while she was in the county jail and then again after Vonda was sent to prison. Hailey had been attempting to play both sides of the fence and it was clear that her loyalty fluctuated with the wind. Here we have a woman desperate to make a name for herself as a writer, inspired by my blog, and reaching out to Vonda's family in hopes of landing fifteen minutes of fame. But Hailey had one big problem: It was already my story.

My work on this case was always meant to free Vonda and to hopefully, possibly find Jessie's actual murderer(s). I am team Vonda. Hailey on the other hand became team Jessie's family. At first glance, these opposing positions seem to make sense… but in all reality, one of them does not.

We have a murder case. Jessie is dead. Vonda is imprisoned. I'm fighting to free Vonda because I believe she's been wrongly convicted. Hailey is fighting for justice for Jessie. I'm no genius, but what the hell is she fighting for exactly? In the eyes of the judicial system and in the eyes of Jessie's family, everyone already got their justice. Hailey argues that Vonda committed this crime and is right where she belongs. Good job beating a dead horse, Hailey.

Vonda might be incarcerated, but she did not commit this crime. She is a victim of a wrongful conviction, as is her family. Wrongful conviction victims are unique in that the injustice that has befallen them actually denies them of their victimhood and in its place is an opposite label, a stain, they must fight against. For most of the wrongfully convicted, their label and identity as a victim is deserved and apparent and we grieve for them and they become our heroes or guardian angels. Being an invisible victim with the label of something evil instead… nobody wants to consider those people, and those types often suffer in silence.

Eventually, I realized that Hailey was never fighting for justice for Jessie or her family. She involved herself in this case to fight me, not because of our supposed differing stances, but because I'd entered the limelight first.

My fight to free Vonda has been constant and consistent since her trial, but over time it has evolved. To understand this, we must walk the ever-winding path of this case, down all the rabbit holes, beyond the trees and through the forest. We must be both biased and unbiased and think like lunatics.

Chapter Two

August 12th, 2016

Friday Morning

Vonda, who had worked at Laughlin Memorial Hospital for roughly twenty-five years, woke up Friday morning on August 12th and went to work. Her job was to process out patients and her shift that day was from 8am to 5pm.

Across town that same morning, Jessie's oldest son, three-year-old Manning, was undergoing oral surgery. Following his surgery, Jessie must have become overwhelmed by the stress of being pregnant, caring for her baby, Sam, and now dealing with her toddler who was probably in pain and cranky from surgery. She sought out Vonda for help. Jessie didn't reach out to her own mother, Susan, for help with the boys; she went to Vonda's work and enlisted her instead. Jessie's actions that morning showcase two important details: number one, she must not have had the best relationship with her mother; and number two, Jessie and Vonda must have shared a close relationship and Jessie must have viewed Vonda as a mother figure for her to feel comfortable going to Vonda's place of employment and asking her to leave work in the middle of her shift. Seeing Jessie needed her, Vonda put Jessie's needs before her own obligations and left work early to help.

Friday Afternoon

Upon leaving work early, Vonda drove her car, following Jessie in her car, to Jessie's boyfriend's place of employment. Once there, John joined his girlfriend and Vonda outside in the parking lot. After chatting a while, Jessie left behind the vehicle she and John shared so that he could drive himself home after work. Jessie and her boys got into Vonda's car with her and they drove to the grocery store.

Friday 3:37pm—3:47pm

Jessie, her boys, and Vonda finished their grocery shopping (which Vonda paid for) and checked out at 3:37pm per their receipt and Food City's surveillance footage. The pair exited the store and made their way out to the car where they loaded the groceries and buckled each boy into their car seat. We do not know what time they ultimately left the parking lot, so we'll allot them 10 minutes for loading groceries and the boys and for them to get situated in the car themselves. With their check-out stamped at 3:37pm and the 10-minute window we gave them to get on the road, we can assume they left the Food City on Snapps Ferry Road in Greeneville around 3:47pm.

Friday 3:57pm—4:02pm

From Food City, Vonda drove the 5.6 miles to Jessie's home on Cross Anchor Park in Greeneville. Based on the area's speed limit, the 5.6 miles should have taken approximately 10 minutes to drive. They would have arrived at Jessie's around 3:57pm. Once at Jessie's, one or both women took the groceries into the house but did not put the groceries away because they were later found still in their bags on the kitchen floor. Obviously, this was an "in and out" situation. We will estimate that this drop off took 5 minutes. Next, they all headed to Vonda's house. We can imagine they left Jessie's around 4:02pm.

Friday 4:02pm–4:10pm

The drive from Jessie's house on Cross Anchor Park in Greeneville to Vonda's house on Davis Valley Road in Afton is 5.1 miles and takes approximately 8 minutes to drive. This would have them arriving at Vonda's around 4:10pm.

Friday 4:10pm

Now at Vonda's, they were greeted by Vonda's husband, Don. The time is now approximately 4:10pm. We do not know how long Jessie stayed at Vonda's, but we do know Vonda gave her $1,000.00 cash to pay Jessie's rent and other bills. We also know that Vonda let Jessie borrow her car to run those errands. I'll go ahead and point this out here and now... many have speculated about Vonda actually giving Jessie that amount of cash or any cash at all, but what no one knows is that she truly did. Months after her conviction, Don asked her during a phone conversation about the title to her car (which was in law enforcement's possession by that time) and Vonda confessed to him that she had sold the title to her car for $1,000.00 because she wanted to help Jessie. So you see, the money from the title was the cash Vonda had given Jessie that day.

Back to the ranch. Jessie left Manning and Sam with Vonda and Don at their house while she went to supposedly pay her bills using Vonda's car. We don't know what time Jessie left their house or what she did after she left (because no bills were ever paid and the cash given to her was never recovered), but she eventually went back to her own house on Cross Anchor Park. During trial testimony, Jessie's neighbor, Patrick, testified to speaking with Jessie outside her home and, a short time later, after he had returned to his own home, he witnessed a white van with two white males arrive at Jessie's. Patrick testified to seeing Jessie get into the white van and leave at roughly 5:30pm.

Friday 6:00pm

The time is now 6:00 and back at Vonda's house her car has magically returned. Vonda and Don's house is positioned atop a hill and their gravel driveway (a fairly steep one, in my opinion) runs down from the front entrance of the house to where it meets the road. Looking at their unmaintained driveway, I would imagine most people who park their car in it would do so down near the bottom, closest to the road, because of the relatively steep grade. That's exactly where Vonda's car was parked upon its return. Although she has said she didn't see clearly who returned her car, Vonda was alerted to its return presumably because she heard a car door shut. Looking out a window, she saw her car parked in the driveway and a white van, possibly two white vans, down in the road near the bottom of her driveway. She stated that she thought she might have seen Jessie's boyfriend, John, but that she wasn't sure.

Seeing that her car was back, Vonda took the opportunity to go pick up her "granddaughter," Jemma, who had been calling Vonda to see where she was and when was she coming to get her. This detail tells us that Vonda had planned to pick up her granddaughter that Friday evening all along and that Jemma had been expecting her. This was not a random or last-minute decision. Jemma is not Vonda and Don's granddaughter by blood or marriage, but they have always treated her as such. Jessie's youngest son wasn't related to them biologically in any way either, but Vonda and Don didn't care, they loved all their "grandchildren" just the same and all the children were frequently in their care.

Vonda left her house to go pick up Jemma and arrived at her destination at 7:00pm. Jemma was in Limestone at her great-grandmother Lillian's house. Lillian testified to Vonda arriving at her home at 7:00pm, stating that she remembered the time because she had been watching television and a new program was just about to start.

The distance between Vonda's house and Lillian's is 19 miles if you take the fastest route, which we'll assume Vonda did. Traveling that distance, going the speed limit and on a Friday evening while the county fair was in town, we will assume the drive took 35 minutes. If Vonda arrived at Lillian's on Charles Humphreys Road in Limestone at 7:00pm and it took her 35 minutes to get there, Vonda likely left her house on Davis Valley Road in Afton at approximately 6:25pm, nearly half an hour after her car had been returned.

When Lillian saw that Vonda had arrived, she and Jemma walked out to Vonda's car to greet her. Lillian and Vonda spent some time chatting before Jemma got into the front passenger seat. Vonda had brought Sam with her and he was seated in his car seat in the back. Vonda, Jemma and Sam all headed back to Vonda's where Don was at home with Manning, who had fallen asleep prior to Vonda leaving to go get Jemma. Assuming the return trip home took roughly the same amount of time as it did to get to Lillian's, and taking into account the unknown amount of time she and Lillian visited, we can guess that Vonda and the kids probably got back to her house between 7:45 and 7:55pm.

Friday 7:30pm

Meanwhile, a man walking his dog along Jud Neal Loop in Afton (just 2 miles or so from Vonda's house) found a body down an embankment that turned out to be Jessie (rest her soul). The man made the discovery at approximately 7:30pm. He returned home, where he allegedly instructed his wife to call 9-1-1.

I have an issue with this man and his discovery. Number one, why did he have his wife call 9-1-1? Why didn't he make the call himself? Can you imagine how that conversation must have gone with the operator? You have the wife calling, the operator answers and then what? Was the guy in the background telling his wife what to say? What if the operator had questions? Did the operator ask the wife, who asked the husband? What's more is that this guy's wife is wheelchair-bound, so unless she happened to already have the phone with her, he would have had to retrieve the phone himself and hand it to his wife, only to have her to call for him! It just doesn't make any sense to me.

Also, what was this guy really doing walking down that road in the first place? I've driven Jud Neal Loop and let me tell you, the entire road is very narrow, even for a single vehicle. And it's extremely rural, think Deliverance-type creepy. Catch my drift? During my drive down Jud Neal Loop, I did spot this guy's house. He and his wife lived in a trailer at the end of the loop and it was up high on a hill, on what looks like potentially several acres of land. So what was this guy doing walking his dog? Most "country folk" out here that live on an acre or more don't walk their dogs because the dogs (my own included) don't freaking need walking… they're free to roam. Seeing the amount of land this guy's house is on really confused me as to why he was walking his dog in the first place.

I'd also love to know whether or not this guy's dog was on a leash. If he was truly, innocently walking his dog that evening and the dog was not on a leash, was it really the dog that found the body? Most unleashed dogs venture ahead of their owners, so I wonder if the dog found the scent before the guy saw what it was. And if the dog was unleashed and found the body, didn't the guy have a difficult time getting his dog away from it? One last interesting tidbit I discovered while touring Jud Neal Loop back in August 2018 is that I spotted a white van parked on this guy's property. Could be something, could be nothing.

Friday Night

Sometime after the 9-1-1 call was made about the discovery, the Greene County Sheriff's Department arrived at the scene, where they ultimately determined it to be a homicide. The following autopsy report details the injuries Jessie suffered:

- Abrasions (cuts and scrapes) and contusions (bruises) on the forehead
- A forehead laceration revealing the skull beneath the abrasion
- A laceration on the right upper eyelid with a 3" by 2" dark purplish-red contusion (bruise) that encircles the swollen right eye and extends to the cheek
- A 2.5" by 1.5" area contusion (bruise) that encircles the left eye
- Pinkish-red contusions and abrasions (cuts and scrapes) on the right cheek
- Blue-colored contusions ranging from 3/8" to 1" scattered across the face with an overlying 3" by 1.5" contusion
- A large 4.5" by 2 1/4" gaping laceration on the posterior (back of) head with the skull fractured underlying the laceration
- A 7/8" purple contusion on the left side of the upper lip
- A 5/16" abrasion/contusion on the right side of the lower lip
- Contusions inside the mouth and on the gums
- Purple-red contusions ranging from 1/2" to 1" on the back of the neck and upper back
- A 1" by 3/4" pink-colored contusion on the right side of the neck
- A 2" by 2.5" blue-colored contusion above the right breast
- A 1.5" by 3/4" contusion on the lower left chest

- A faint pink and roughly circular lesion (wound) on the left side of the abdomen measuring 1 1/4" by 1 1/16"
- Two reddish-purple contusions on the right side of the upper back and right shoulder measuring 5.5" by 3" and 3.5" by 2" respectively
- A 1/4" abrasion on the lower back
- A 1 3/8" abrasion on the right upper arm with a 3/4" faint blue contusion
- A 3/4" pink contusion on the right forearm
- Multiple blue and pink contusions on the right forearm ranging in size from 1/8" to 1.5" on the back of the right hand and fingers
- A 5/8" orange-colored abrasion on the right hand
- A fractured ring finger on the right hand
- A 3/16" abrasion on the interior of the right thumb
- A blue-colored 1/2" contusion on the front of the left shoulder
- Reddish-orange abrasions on the back of the left upper arm and ranging in size from 1/4" to 1/2"
- Contusions on the inside bend of the elbow of the left arm
- A 1 3/4" by 1" blue contusion on the front of the left forearm
- Small hemorrhages (spots of bleeding under the skin) on the front of the left wrist and left hand
- The back of the left hand and fingers have 1/4" to 2.5" purple contusions and red abrasions measuring 1/16" to 1/8"

- Purple contusions on the palm of the left hand ranging from 3/8" to 1"

- A 4 3/4" by 5/8" blue contusion on the top right thigh with a 2 3/4" by 1.5" red abrasion

- A 4" by 1/2" yellowish abrasion on the back of the right thigh and a 2" by 3/8" reddish-orange abrasion on the inside of the right thigh

- 1/16" to 1.5" contusions on the front of the right lower leg along with abrasions ranging in size from 3/8" to 2"

- Cause of death: blunt force trauma

An estimated time of death was never established nor recorded.

No weapon was positively identified or ever recovered. No witnesses either. DNA found underneath Jessie's fingernails belonged to three unidentified males. DNA found in Jessie's underwear belonged to three males. One DNA sample belonged to her boyfriend, John. The second DNA sample from her underwear belonged to an unknown male. The third DNA sample was identified as JT's, John's father. Due to the sample only being a partial, it could not be conclusively determined as being JT's. Father and son share similar DNA and when the DNA sample isn't "strong enough" to register as being one hundred percent belonging to a specific individual, a partial sample only reveals just enough of a DNA profile to ascertain it belonging to a particular DNA family.

Think of it this way, let's say John's DNA is represented by a famous painting, "Painting A," and JT's DNA is represented by a second famous painting, "Painting B." Although Painting A and Painting B are different works of art, they were both painted by the same artist and so we can expect the styles to be similar, much like John and JT's DNA. When you stand back in view of the entire painting you can clearly identify it as either Painting A or Painting B, but if you only view one square inch of the painting (a partial piece), it would be difficult to determine if you were viewing Painting A (John's DNA) or Painting B (JT's DNA) due to the fact that the brush strokes (genetic make-up) of each painting are so similar.

I'd now like to offer my reasoning for including the results of the autopsy report. I feel that sharing the details will help illustrate the amount and degree of the injuries Jessie sustained. I will now point out a few more details to consider.

Both the defense and the prosecution, including the pathologist, all agreed that some of Jessie's injuries were consistent with defensive wounds. This means Jessie fought for her life, possibly even maiming her attacker(s).

Former Greene County Deputy Danny Ricker testified at the trial that there were no visible scratches, bruises or markings on Vonda when the sheriff and deputies arrived at her home hours after being called to the crime scene. Additionally, Vonda's DNA was never found on the victim or at the crime scene. There was, however, DNA of an unknown female found.

Something else to consider is the physical comparison of Jessie and Vonda. Jessie was 21 years old at the time of her death and was approximately 5'8"-5'9," weighing roughly 150 pounds give or take a few, and had been physically active just a couple years before, during high school. Let us also not disregard the adrenaline and strength of a mother in "mama bear" mode. Jessie's friends and family will tell you that she was a fighter in every sense of the word. She was strong, brave and wouldn't hesitate to stomp anyone's ass if they deserved it. Her uncle was quoted in the local newspaper, The Greeneville Sun, referring to his niece as "a spitfire."

Vonda, on the other hand, was not a spitfire. She was approximately 52 years old, weighed roughly 200-plus pounds at the time of Jessie's death, and is only 4'11." Vonda was not physically active at the time, nor had she been in the several years prior to the incident. If Jessie and Vonda ever found themselves on the inside of a ring, it wouldn't be a fair fight, Jessie would be the winner without effort.

Friday 10:00pm—11:00pm

Sometime between 10:00pm and 11:00pm the night of Jessie's murder, her mother, Susan, showed up at Vonda's house looking for her daughter. Susan told Vonda that Jessie wasn't at home and hadn't been answering her phone. Vonda told Susan that the last time she had seen Jessie was around 4:30pm when Jessie borrowed her car. Susan left Jessie's children at Vonda's and apparently went elsewhere to look for Jessie.

The Next Morning
August 13th

Saturday, 2:00am

In the early morning hours of the next day, Vonda's household was awakened by Sheriff Pat Hankins and two of his deputies, Buddy Randolph and Danny Ricker, knocking on Vonda's door. Vonda opened the door and stepped outside with them. At this time, and for the duration of their visit, Deputy Danny Ricker was recording audio. In the audio recording, which was later played at the trial, you could hear Vonda's husband, Don, open the front door and ask Vonda what the sheriff and deputies wanted. Vonda then replied by telling Don that they wanted to search the car. Next, you heard either the sheriff or one of the deputies ask Vonda how to open the trunk of the car. Vonda could be heard explaining to them that they have to pull a lever inside the vehicle, next to the driver's seat, which one of them did. The opening and closing of car doors is audible in the recording. After searching the car, they told Vonda that the vehicle would be impounded because of some "stuff" they found in it, to which Vonda readily consented.

Interestingly, during the trial, Danny Ricker testified under oath that they did not open the car prior to sealing it as evidence. Yet, when his own audio recording was played for the courtroom to hear, it was clear that they did open the car and search it, possibly contaminating any evidence.

The man who arrived at Vonda's house to tow her car to TBI (Tennessee Bureau of Investigation) in Knoxville was Troy. Troy suddenly passed away at the age of 52 on March 27th, 2018, just two months before Vonda's trial. Amazingly enough, Deputy Danny Ricker had been demoted to civil process server (a paper-pusher position) in the middle of the case and Detective Buddy Randolph had retired prior to the trial. Interestingly, Sheriff Pat Hankins never took the stand.

Shortly after Jessie's death, Vonda was determined to find out what had happened to Jessie and who did it. On an October day in 2016, just two months following the murder, Vonda decided to do some investigating of her own. She had a gut feeling that those white vans had something to do with it, so she spent that day traveling around and asking questions. Evidently, she either asked the wrong person or caught the attention of an enemy.

When Vonda returned home from her day of detective work, her husband asked her if she would run to the store for some snacks. Doting woman that she was, she went out to do just that. On her drive back home from the store, she noticed blue lights flashing behind her in the darkness. Her immediate thought was that she was being pulled over because she must have had a taillight out. She pulled over on the shoulder of the road, put the car in park, rolled down her driver's window and then leaned over to the passenger seat to dig through her purse for her driver license.

Prepared to greet the officer and hand over her license, a fist shot through the open window and hit her square in the eye. The blue lights were gone. A man opened her car door and pulled her to the ground. Vonda was repeatedly punched and kicked by two men and, while lying on the ground being beaten, she saw a truck parked behind her car and an unfamiliar woman standing next to it. Vonda recognized one of the men and would later allegedly confide in her daughter-in-law that it was Jessie's boyfriend, John. Vonda claims that John told her to stop asking questions about the white vans and if she didn't keep her mouth shut, he would hurt Manning. The two men allegedly attempted to lift Vonda into their truck but were unsuccessful. Vonda blacked out.

Back at home, Don was beginning to worry about his wife, who hadn't come back from the store yet. He decided to call the police. Vonda's car was located easily enough by law enforcement and was found right where she'd left it, parked on the shoulder of the road and still running, but with no Vonda in it.

Family was alerted to her disappearance and a search party formed that chilly October night to find her. The search party consisted of family and members of the Greene County Sheriff's Department, including Detective Buddy Randolph. The search was unsuccessful that night but, before it concluded, one individual Freudian-slipped a comment to Vonda's daughter-in-law. Buddy Randolph allegedly made the strange suggestion that perhaps Vonda had jumped off a bridge… insinuating that she had committed suicide.

The following morning, a woman driving down that same road that Vonda had disappeared from the night before saw a body in a ditch not far from a bridge. It was Vonda. Once more, the family raced to the scene, which was 1/4 mile down the road from where her car had been found. She was taken by ambulance to the very hospital she worked at, Laughlin Memorial.

Vonda was taken to the ICU, where she spent the next week or two recovering from a concussion, fractured ribs, a black eye and other more minor injuries. At some point, she had either been intubated or there was a failed attempt to intubate because her throat was sore from the procedure and she couldn't really speak.

Soon enough in came Detective Buddy Randolph. He claimed to be there to take an official statement from Vonda, but she refused to give one. She had been threatened, beaten and left for dead, and from that moment on she would do as she was warned and keep her mouth shut to protect Manning. Many skeptics suggest Vonda's disappearance and beating never happened, including my rival, Hailey. They all want to believe that Vonda and her entire family, even the stranger who initially spotted Vonda in the ditch, are lying. Adding fuel to the skeptics' accusation is the fact that there is no police report about this incident. Hailey, in particular, has enjoyed pointing that out. Due to there not being an existing police report, this entire incident must have been fabricated. What Hailey's wool-covered eyes and inside-the-box brain can't comprehend is that there's no police report due to the obvious cover up. This was the first instance Vonda was nearly killed over this case, but it wouldn't be the last.

Chapter Three

Listen, here's the deal... I gotta change gears. We're gonna go off-roading with these next few chapters. I set the stage all pretty-like with Chapters One and Two, but now it's time to get dirty. There might be some foul language ahead, beer drinking, chain smoking and grammar my editor will want to charge me double to deal with. Why is this happening? Because this case is not what meets the eye and, therefore, this book cannot be either. Understand? Good. Let's do this.

In this Chapter, I'll introduce you to some of our players, but first let's go over what makes a player a "player." My mom and I chose the term "player" to describe a person of interest or someone we think is relevant to this story. A player is not necessarily a murder suspect. Some players we consider possible suspects, some we consider possible accomplices and, above all, we think most of the players on our list possibly know something about the circumstances of Jessie's death. Did you catch all the "possibles" and "possiblys" in there? Those are part of my disclaimer, which delicately shouts, "I have no idea if any of these people were involved with this crime and there is no proof whatsoever of their involvement in any way, so please don't sue my ass."

I now hereby declare all you lucky ducks reading this... my sleuths. Welcome to the club. As a sleuth in this case, your job is to read and consider everything I put before you and to help free Vonda and deliver Jessie justice by untangling this mess and connecting the dots. Who killed Jessie? There are numerous clues along the way, some of which will lead us down rabbit holes, but don't be discouraged... even seemingly wrong turns down rabbit holes can offer clues of their own. The thing to remember is to try to be aware you're down a rabbit hole when you are and then come out of it.... Don't get sucked in and stay there. Ever hear the saying, "can't see the forest for the trees"? This idiom undeniably applies to this case. There are dozens of trees we must consider, but we must not get lost in them. We must periodically step back in view of the forest. Conversely, we must also recognize the trees for the forest. Sometimes taking a closer look at the bigger picture is what's needed. My final piece of advice before we start is to always be aware of your sleuth hat. Just as I've asked you to become a sleuth with this case, I ask you to be a sleuth with some of my writing. You might need to read between the lines every now and then or work to decipher what I'm saying without being able to say. The reason for my occasional use of imagery and coded language is for my safety. So stay sharp, my sleuths! Now let's crack a cold beer and set the stage for our players.

I was born in Denver, raised in Orlando. I moved to Long Island, NY with a best friend when I was twenty-one, where we lived in the back of a Bulgarian artist's studio for a short time. We ultimately spent a couple of days and nights homeless after our stay at the studio had run out. We found ourselves wandering the streets of New York City one night with a bottle of vodka and the world at our fingertips. We wandered Central Park in the wee hours of that chilly October morning until we came upon the ice rink. There was a wooden fence enclosing the area next to the bleachers where hot air from some machine was expelled via a fan or pump of some type. We jumped that fence around 3am and pressed our backs to where the hot air came blowing out. The blast of heat came at maybe two-minute intervals and lasted about 30-45 seconds... enough to keep us somewhat warm in the cold night air. We somehow slept there like that, leaning on one another, for a few hours. Before I knew it, the sun was rising and we heard people talking. We peeked through the fence and saw a few park rangers of sorts, just a few yards from the fence. In our infinite 21-year-old wisdom, we determined that we should make a break for it, so we clambered over the fence opposite the side the park rangers were standing near and ran for it. We ran through Central Park early on that cold October morning, with the sun rising the most beautiful orange and pink colors you could ever hope to see. We ran among all of this brilliance and among frost-covered everything and I never felt more alive in my entire life. All the energies of New York City were with me that magic morning... the new, the old, the historic... I felt all of them all at once.

    I soon moved back to Orlando. There, I navigated O-Town and Miami and painted the towns red doing so. Orlando was my playground and I loved every bit of it. My fun came to a halt in the check-out lane of a Publix. There was a bird flying around the store that summer and it wouldn't leave me be. It was swooping at me down the aisles and nearly hit me while I was checking out. When I got home, the bird had brought the news before the pink plus sign had the chance to appear. I was pregnant.

    Four years later and I bought a travel trailer. I threw a dart at a map and it hit a quaint little town in South Carolina. I packed my four-year-old in my car, along with our belongings, and haphazardly moved to a new state, where we would live for six months in our travel trailer in a campground. We had a wonderful life there, but I met someone. We ended up moving to East Tennessee, where my new boyfriend was born and raised. We lived in our travel trailer in his parents' backyard for a year before finally moving into our own home. And that is how I came to be in Tennessee and that is how I met Vonda. My boyfriend became my husband and his family became mine.

Greene County is a beautiful place. The entire Appalachian region can easily be described as God's country because of its beauty. Tree-covered mountains give way to valleys of green grass and, left un-mowed, wildflowers grow and bloom, adding whimsy to the scenery. Those valleys roll with hills. Stretching farther away from the mountains, the landscape becomes "the country." This is where we live… out in the country. Fields and farms surround us and, twice a year, after farmers have cut hay, giant rolls of round bales dot the landscape. Winding back roads litter the county and are best driven with a cold beer in hand. There's no shortage of old farmhouses outfitted with rocking chairs on their porches. This is where we drink our sweet tea, cold beer and moonshine. The porch is where life is lived out in the country, unless you're out in the fields working. Life is slow and steady and the changing of seasons is really what signals the passing of time.

Appalachia is a magical place and still offers that old-world charm of days gone by. The modern world co-exists here alongside the old ways and many who live here have never moved away. Generations of families have lived in the region dating back hundreds of years. Outsiders are generally viewed with some suspicion and not many like a Yankee. It was once suggested to me that I tell people I was from Denver rather than saying I was from Florida because locals might assume I was actually a transplant from New York, rather than a true Floridian. Small town mentality hit me like a foreign brick to the face. For a girl who had some traveling under her belt and who was raised in a city, it took me quite some time to adjust to country life in Greene County. Just as I had finally begun to embrace the region and the lifestyle and to carve out a piece of it to call my own, Vonda was sentenced to prison for life.

I spent my days thereafter getting acquainted with the devil's playground in an intimate way, and once aware of it there was no turning a blind eye to what hides beneath the beauty.

    At the start of our amateur investigation, my mom and I turned to Facebook to snoop on people. We'd begin by looking through their personal information they had publicly listed on their profile and then we'd move on to their friends list if it was visible. If the individual we were looking at was a potential suspect in our minds, we scrolled through all their publicly available posts, some of which dated back several years. Mostly we were interested in any posts from 2016, as that was the year Jessie died. More specifically, we zeroed in on any posts that were made in August through December of 2016. We not only read any posts we felt might be relevant to our investigation, we read all the comments and scanned through any "likes" the post had gotten. The friends lists, particularly, were a great help. By viewing everyone's friends, we gained a pretty good idea of who knew who and we were also able to figure out who was related to who. This could be incredibly time consuming if an individual had more than three hundred friends. We would frequently become distracted by some of the people we found on these friends lists and find ourselves slipping down a rabbit hole because we'd clicked on the friend's Facebook profile and gotten lost looking through that one.

    The amount of ghetto-ass people we found and their trashy Facebook profiles we scoured is enough to blow your fucking socks off. I have seen things I can't un-see and I have learned things about the area I live in that I can't unlearn. When I'm snooping through Facebook, it feels every bit like being in the twilight zone.

    The region is riddled with drugs. Opioid use (painkillers) in Tennessee might make national headlines from time to time, but meth is the more popular drug of choice these days, and it's one hell of a money maker. East Tennessee has a long history with drugs. Back in the '60s it was marijuana and in the '70s and '80s it was cocaine. The '90s and early 2000s ushered in pills (painkillers, muscle relaxers, etc.) and heroin. Next came meth. In the early days of meth use in the region, it was being cooked in little pop-up places like vans, shacks, barns and trailer homes. The locals were making it themselves and the amount being distributed wasn't very significant. More recently, however, much larger quantities of meth are being distributed and the number of meth heads around town has dramatically increased. I can probably count on seeing a handful of them during any given trip to town.

The meth currently infiltrating Greene County isn't being cooked by locals, it's coming in from Mexico. Apparently, this Mexican meth is all the rage. I've heard tales of it being manufactured in a large facility in Mexico, where it inevitably makes its way across the border, over to a hub in Atlanta and then up to East Tennessee.

I've also heard rumors that shipments of meth are delivered in the trailers of semi-trucks from Atlanta to the truck stop in Baileyton, not far from where I live. An acquaintance of my husband's told me once that these trucks park at the Baileyton truck stop and are sometimes "searched" by police. It's rumored that the police then allegedly confiscate the drugs and the drug money for themselves. This same acquaintance went on to say that a law enforcement buddy of his also told him that the situation with the cops confiscating and then distributing the meth is so bad that the damn drug dogs go after the police cruisers and have to be pulled away from them. That, ladies and gentlemen, is our stage. It's a small town, a devil's playground.

Without further ado, let us go over our players, shall we?

VONDA

Approximately 52 years old at time of conviction

Married to Don

Mother to Wyatt and Curtis

Lived on Davis Valley Road in Afton

Biological grandmother to Manning

Grandmother figure to Manning's brother, Sam

Grandmother figure to Jemma

Arrested for the murder of Jessie in March 2017

Convicted in May 2018

Sentenced to life in prison

Charges: one count first degree murder for the death of Jessie, one count second degree murder for the death of Jessie's unborn baby

Vonda's attorney—Steven

No prior arrests

JESSIE

21 years old at the time of death

Was in a relationship with John

Mother to Manning and Sam

Approximately 16 weeks pregnant at the time of death

Daughter of Susan

Lived on Cross Anchor Park in Greeneville

Found murdered on Jud Neal Loop in Afton

Died Friday, August 12th, 2016

No public arrest records (that I could find)

"SUSAN"

Approximately 47 years old at the time of her daughter's death

Mother to Jessie

Biological grandmother to Manning and Sam

Lives in Rogersville

Public records include arrests for driving under the influence, reckless endangerment (she was driving drunk with Manning and Sam in the vehicle), open alcohol container violation, DWI (driving under the influence of drugs), public drunkenness, child restraint violation, 2 separate violations for driving with a suspended license, 3 unknown criminal charges

"JOHN"

Approximately 25 years old at the time of his girlfriend's death

Son of JT and Linda

Brother to Benjamin

Lived in Greeneville with Jessie, her sons, and his father, JT, on Cross Anchor Park

Ex-girlfriends include: Nicole and Britney

Father to Britney's son

Married Christy in February 2018

Had a son with Christy in August 2018

Public arrest record indicates an arrest for assault in June 2017. Per the Greeneville Sun's article about the incident, John allegedly fractured a young woman's skull

"JT"

Approximately 45 years old at the time of Jessie's death

Divorced from Linda

Father of John and Benjamin

Friends with Bradley

Lived with John and Jessie and her kids on Cross Anchor Park in Greeneville

Currently serving time for involvement in a meth distribution conspiracy during a multiagency drug bust in October 2018

Was borrowed from his jail cell in the Greene County Detention Center and used as a witness for the prosecution during Vonda's trial

Public records indicate arrests for meth distribution conspiracy, charges included possession of a firearm, furtherance of a drug trafficking crime, distribution, possession with the intent to distribute and money laundering. Prior arrests include possession of a firearm with intent to go armed (dangerous felony), manufacturing meth, delivering meth, sale of meth, unlawful drug paraphernalia use and activities, 2 separate offenses for burglary of a dwelling, 7 separate offenses of theft, violation of probation, contraband in a penal facility, unlawful telecommunication devices in a penal facility, driving with a revoked license, unlawful possession of a weapon, unlawful possession of a knife with a blade over four inches, failure to appear, and harassment

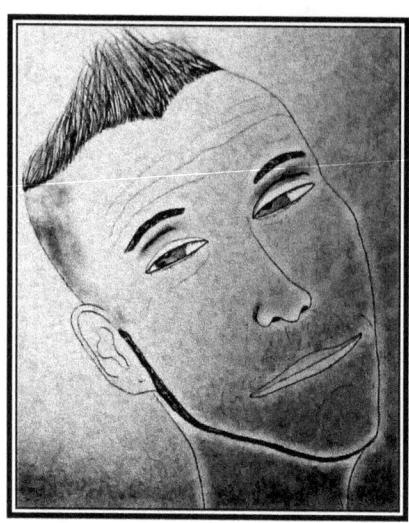

"BENJAMIN"

Approximately 19 years old at the time of Jessie's death

Brother to John

Son of JT and Linda

Owned a white van at the time of Jessie's death

Rumored to have spent some time also living in the trailer on Cross Anchor Park with John, JT, Jessie, and Jessie's boys.

Public records indicate arrests for aggravated cruelty to animals (in December 2017, dead cats and dogs were found inside and outside the home Benjamin lived in with his mother, Linda), 3 separate instances of violation of probation, schedule II drugs, manufacturing, delivering, possession, sale, driving with a suspended license, possession of unlawful drug paraphernalia use and activities, and 4 separate instances of theft

"BRADLEY"

Approximately 33 years old at the time of Jessie's death

Friends with JT and most other players on our list

Public records indicate arrests for theft of property between $2,500-$10,000, kidnapping, domestic assault, failure to appear, 2 separate instances of probation violation offenses, possession/casual exchange, possession of unlawful drug paraphernalia use and activities, schedule IV drugs: manufacturing/delivery/sell, other thefts of property, another possession of drug paraphernalia, expired registration, aggravated burglary of a building/habitation, domestic assault, possession of drugs for manufacturing/delivery or sell, 8 separate unknown criminal offenses, public intoxication, theft of merchandise

"LINDA"

Approximately 43 years old at the time of Jessie's death

Ex-wife of JT

Mother to Benjamin and John

Friends with many of the players on this list

Public records indicate arrests for aggravated animal cruelty, 2 separate probation violation offenses, simple possession/casual exchange, assault, 3 separate offenses for financial responsibility law, domestic assault, failure to appear, meth—possession/casual exchange, other simple possession/casual exchange, possession of unlawful drug paraphernalia use and activity, driving without a license, another probation violation, 10 separate unknown criminal charges

"WYATT"

Approximately 32 years old at the time of Jessie's death

Son of Vonda and Don

Brother to Curtis

Dated Jessie in 2012 or 2013, which resulted in the birth of Manning

Dated "Black Eyes"

Dated Jemma's mom, Janet

At one point, was friends or acquaintances with Susan, Black Eyes, Nicole and Adam

No public arrest records (that I could find)

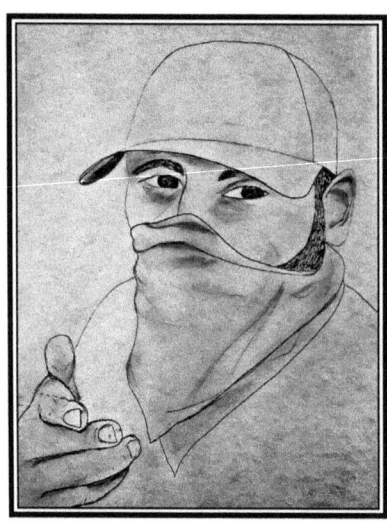

"SHANE"

Approximately 27 years old at the time of Jessie's death

Dated Jessie in 2014 or 2015, which resulted in the birth of Sam

Friends with the majority of players on this list

Public records indicate arrests for interference with an emergency telephone call, assault with bodily injury, criminal trespassing, driving while license revoked, domestic assault, theft up to $1,000, failure to appear, probation violation, resisting stop/arrest/search, 3 counts of assault (physical contact), DUI, meth—possession or casual exchange, simple possession/casual exchange, possession of unlawful drug paraphernalia use and activity, other probation violations, failure to appear, criminal impersonation, another possession of unlawful drug paraphernalia use and activity, theft up to $1,000, contempt of court, another domestic assault, at least 3 possessions of drug paraphernalia, simple possession/casual exchange, aggravated assault, financial responsibility law, expired registration, vandalism, criminal trespassing, public intoxication, theft of merchandise, 7 separate unknown charges

"CHRISTY"

Approximately 20-something years old at the time of Jessie's death

Married to John

Mother of John's son

Friends with Benjamin and a couple of players on this list

Long time family friend of John's family

No public arrest records (that I could find)

"TRAVIS"

Approximately 26 years old at the time of Jessie's death

Rumored to have lived on Jud Neal Loop at the time of Jessie's death

Friends with many players on this list

Public records include arrests for probation violation, another probation violation, 2 DUIs, financial responsibility law, driving with a license that was suspended/cancelled/or revoked

"LEE"

Approximately 46 years old at the time of Jessie's death

Lived on Jud Neal Loop at the time of Jessie's death

Friends with Bradley

Arrested and charged with attempted first-degree murder, felony counts of reckless endangerment, rape and aggravated kidnapping in July 2017; still awaiting trial as of July 2019

"MIRANDA"

Approximately 22 years old at the time of Jessie's death

Close friends with Bradley and friends with many players on this list

Lived on Tyne Gray Road at the time of Jessie's death

Public records indicate arrests for criminal impersonation, at least 5 probation violations, simple possession/casual exchange, public intoxication, possession of unlawful drug paraphernalia use and activity, contempt of court, failure to appear, evading arrest (risk of death or injury), aggravated assault, another evading arrest, reckless endangerment-vehicle/felony, tampering with evidence, throwing objects/shooting at transportation, driving on the wrong side of the road, criminal littering, other possessions of drug paraphernalia, 2 domestic assaults, theft of merchandise, simple possession of a controlled substance/casual exchange, 7 separate unknown charges, accessory after the fact

The accessory after the fact charge is for Miranda allegedly aiding an inmate escape

"BRITNEY"

Approximately 22 years old at the time of Jessie's death

Once dated John, which resulted in the birth of a baby boy born in February 2016 (just six months before Jessie's death)

Currently dating Brendon (as of July 2019)

Was close with JT

Friends with many players on this list

Public records indicate arrests for meth—possession or casual exchange, simple possession and casual exchange, possession of unlawful drug paraphernalia use and activity, vandalism up to $1,000, 3 separate probation violation offenses, financial responsibility law, robbery

"BRENDON"

Approximately 32 years old at the time of Jessie's death

Dating Britney (as of July 2019)

Friends with the majority of players on this list

Public records indicate arrests for at least 3 probation violations, meth—manufacturing/delivery/sell/possession with intent, 2 possessions of unlawful drug paraphernalia use and activity, simple possession/casual exchange, 2 joyriding—unauthorized use of auto/other vehicles, multiple possessions of unlawful drug paraphernalia use and activity, 2 counts of assault—threat of bodily injury, another meth—manufacturing/delivery/sell/possession with intent, criminal impersonation, unlawful removal/alteration of registration tag, financial responsibility, unlicensed/unregistered vehicle on highway/occupy unregistered mobile home, muffler law, 2 DUIs, driving while license is suspended, evading arrest, theft up to $500, reckless endangerment—vehicle misdemeanor, at least 3 criminal impersonations, 2 failures to appear, domestic assault, driving on revoked/suspended/allowing unlicensed driver to drive, leaving the scene of an accident with property damage, meth—manufacturing/delivery/sale/possession with intent, theft of property, assault of a police officer, resisting arrest or obstruction of a legal process, theft of property up to $1,000, 2 aggravated assaults, resisting stop/arrest, revoked license, reckless endangerment, kidnapping, felony evading arrest, evading arrest (risk of death), 11 separate unknown charges

"NICOLE"

Approximately 26 years old at the time of Jessie's death

Once dated John and Damien

Friends with most players on this list

No public arrest records (that I could find)

"DAMIEN"

Approximately 25 years old at the time of Jessie's death

Once dated Nicole

Friends with most players on this list

Public records indicate arrests for 2 counts of schedule III drugs: manufacturing/delivery/sell/possession, probation violation, contraband in a penal facility (conspiracy), schedule IV drugs: manufacturing/delivery/sell/possession, at least 3 possessions of unlawful drug paraphernalia use and activity, meth—possession or casual exchange, domestic assault, driving while license is suspended, at least 3 counts of simple possession/casual exchange, meth—possession or casual exchange, possession of unlawful drug paraphernalia use and activity, 3 DUIs, possession of or for manufacturing/delivery/or sale, public intoxication, 2 driving on revoked/suspended/allowing unlicensed driver to drive, reckless endangerment, evading arrest, possession of drug paraphernalia, public intoxication

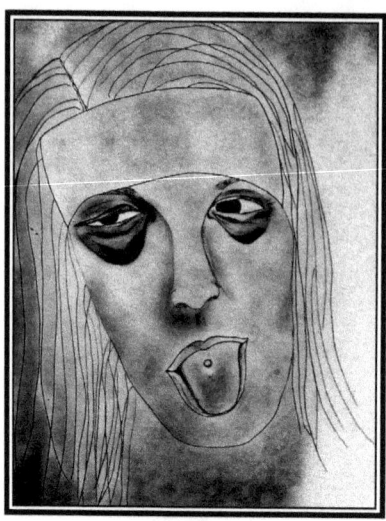

"BLACK EYES"

Approximately 29 years old at the time of Jessie's death

Once dated Wyatt

Friends with most players on this list

Public arrest records indicate arrests for possession of unlawful drug paraphernalia use and activity, possession of a firearm with intent to go armed (dangerous felony), meth—manufacturing/delivery/sale/possession with intent

"CHASITY"

Approximately 25 years old at the time of Jessie's death

In a relationship with Cody (as of July 2019)

Friends with many players on this list

Public records indicate arrests for meth—possession or casual exchange, 5 counts of probation violation, possession of unlawful drug paraphernalia use and activity, failure to appear, obedience to any traffic control device, financial responsibility law, theft up to $500, driving while license revoked

Indicted on October 10th 2018 in a meth distribution conspiracy

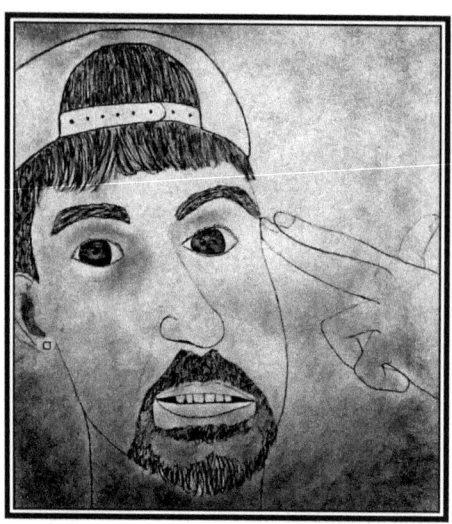

"CODY"

Approximately 22 years old at the time of Jessie's death

Dating Chasity (as of July 2019)

Friends with a couple of players on this list

Public records indicate arrests for at least 3 probation violations, financial responsibility law, driving while license suspended, evading arrest, resisting stop/arrest/search, meth—possession or casual exchange, employ firearm with intent to go armed (dangerous felony), theft of property from $2,500-$10,000, unlawful possession without prescription, possession of unlawful drug paraphernalia use and activity, speeding, 2 possessions of or for manufacturing/delivery/or sale, at least 2 possessions of drug paraphernalia

"C.R."

- Approximately 40 years old at the time of Jessie's death
- Rumored to have lived on Cross Anchor Park (the same trailer park where Jessie, John and JT lived) at the time of Jessie's death
- Friends with nearly everyone on this player list and many other alleged "bad guys"
- Public records indicate arrests for financial responsibility, vehicular assault, DUI, 3 counts of simple possession/contraband substance/casual exchange/distribution, probation violation, 3 separate counts for possession with intent to manufacture/deliver/sell, aggravated assault, theft of property, simple possession and casual exchange, 30 separate unknown charges—system only reads "See Rule Docket For Charge"

"DAWN"

Approximately 31 years old at the time of Jessie's death

Rumored to have lived very near Vonda at the time of Jessie's death

Rumored to have "freaked out" one night about Jessie's death and allegedly became paranoid about the circumstances surrounding her death

Close friends with Litt and friends with many other players on this list

Public records indicate 2 arrests for meth—manufacturing/delivery/sale/possession with intent, at least 5 possessions of unlawful drug paraphernalia use and activity, simple possession/casual exchange, failure to appear, possession/sell/barter/give away legend drug, 3 schedule II drugs-manufacturing/delivery/sell/possession, driving while license suspended, schedule IV drugs—manufacturing/delivery/sell/possession, unlawful possession without prescription, contraband in penal facility, theft up to $1,000, open container, possession of unlawful drug paraphernalia use and activity, at least 2 possessions of drug paraphernalia, public intoxication, possession of or for manufacturing/

delivery/or sale, child endangerment/abuse/neglect, 2 thefts of property, forgery, driving without a license, failure to appear, theft of merchandise, driving on a revoked/suspended/allowing an unlicensed driver to drive, DUI, 5 separate unknown charges

"LITT"

Approximately 20-something years old at the time of Jessie's death

Close friends with Dawn and friends with many others on this player list

Public records indicate arrests for meth—possession or casual exchange, 2 possessions of unlawful drug paraphernalia use and activity, DUI, 2 driving while license is suspended, 2 simple possession/casual exchanges, possession of unlawful drug paraphernalia use and activity, 3 counts of probation violation, 2 failures to appear, felony evading arrest, meth—manufacturing/delivery/sale/possession with intent, reckless driving, 2 possession of drug paraphernalia, 2 simple possessions of a controlled substance/casual exchange/distribution, 2 domestic assaults, joyriding- unauthorized use of auto/other vehicles, 2 financial responsibility law, 2 driving without a license, reckless endangerment, 2 counts of child restraint, speeding

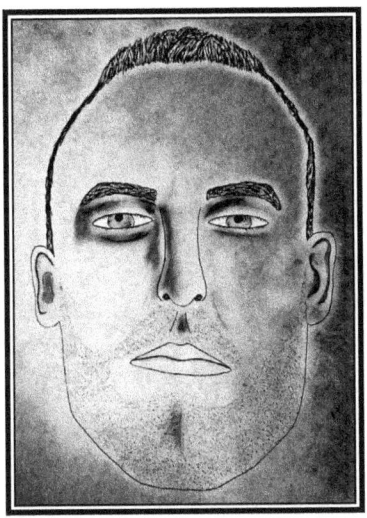

"ADAM"

Approximately 27 years old at the time of Jessie's death

Once either dated Jessie or casually hooked up with her

Son of Susan's friend who lives on Old Baileyton Road

Public records indicate arrests for joyriding—unauthorized use of auto/other vehicles, 2 implied consents, 2 DUIs, possession of unlawful drug paraphernalia use and activity, mutilated plates must be replaced, speeding, driving while license revoked, 2 financial responsibility laws, 2 registration certificate must be carried, 2 driver license must be carried and exhibited, evading arrest, bumper law, theft of property (possession of stolen property)

Chapter Four

Here is where we get into the behind-the-scenes shit. Crack a cold beer, sleuths, and hang onto your hats. You can refer to Chapter Three and our player profiles when you need a face to a name. Now let's go back over the timeline in more detail and, while we're at it, we'll play devil's advocate. But first, let's go over some facts.

- Fact #1 No murder weapon was ever found, let alone identified

- Fact #2 Vonda's DNA was not found on Jessie or at the crime scene (despite the DNA of multiple others being found)

- Fact #3 Vonda did not have any bruises, scrapes, scratches or marks on her body (she clearly would have had at least something because both the prosecution and the defense agreed that Jessie fought for her life against her attacker)

- Fact #4 is debatable as a "fact," but Vonda had no true motive to murder Jessie and I think we can accept that as a fact because Vonda's actions that day and leading to that day do not suggest she wanted to kill Jessie (i.e.: financially helping with Jessie's rent, bills and cost of schooling, taking care of and providing for Jessie and her two sons, leaving work early that day to help Jessie with her boys, taking them grocery shopping, giving Jessie money that very day to go pay bills and allowing Jessie to borrow her car)

- Fact #5 If Vonda did murder Jessie, she would have had to do it with Jessie's children present and neither child displayed any signs or behavior that would have been indicative of experiencing such trauma

- Fact #6 Authorities cannot explain how or when Jessie's blood came to be in Vonda's car

- Fact #7 Detectives who initially searched Vonda's car prior to sealing it as evidence later testified that they did not open the vehicle that night, despite an audio recording proving otherwise

- Fact #8 Vonda did not turn herself in, yet the Greene County Sheriff's Department announced that she had

- Fact #9 Lillian testified to Vonda arriving at her home around 7:00pm and not seeing any blood in Vonda's vehicle at that time (Jessie's body was found at approximately 7:30pm)

- Fact #10 Vonda's behavior/composure both before and after Jessie's death never suggested she was planning on committing a murder or that she had committed murder

- Fact #11 During the trial, Vonda was never evaluated by a mental health professional to determine if in fact she displayed any signs of obsessive behavior or tendencies in relationships, which is the basis of the motive the prosecution put forward. Her "motive" would have rested solely on her mental health... but no one evaluated her for confirmation, and therefore the motive is not credible so I piss on it

- Fact #12 An estimated time of death was never recorded, which is vital information
- Fact #13 Judge Dugger denied DNA testing be done on the fetus, which is also vital information

If you are even slightly familiar with murder cases (possibly from true crime shows, films or books) then you have an understanding that there are three major components for a conviction:

1) DNA/physical evidence
2) Weapon
3) Confession

In this case, all three elements are missing, including a rational motive to justify murdering your grandson's young, pregnant mother who you were close with and cared for.

Now back to our timeline, sleuths! Let's begin at Food City where Vonda took Jessie and her sons grocery shopping. They checked out at approximately 3:37pm. After walking out to the car, loading the groceries, buckling both kids into their car seats and settling themselves in... let's say they left Food City around 3:47pm.

ARRIVING AT JESSIE'S
The route Vonda most likely traveled to get to Jessie's place in Cross Anchor would have taken approximately 10 minutes driving the speed limit, which we will assume Vonda did, as she

was not known to speed. They likely arrived at Jessie's place around 3:57pm.

LEAVING JESSIE'S
After arriving at Jessie's and putting the groceries inside, which we will allot 5 minutes for, we will imagine they all left Jessie's around 4:02pm.

ARRIVING AT VONDA'S
The route Vonda most likely took to travel from Jessie's place to her own home on Davis Valley Road should have taken approximately 8 minutes. We will imagine they arrived at Vonda's house around 4:10pm, where Vonda's husband, Don, was at home. We do not know how long Jessie was at Vonda's house before borrowing Vonda's car and some cash to go pay her bills.

JESSIE'S PLACE 5:30pm
Whatever time Jessie left Vonda's house, leaving both of her sons in Vonda's care, Jessie resurfaces at her place in Cross Anchor a bit before 5:30pm. Her neighbor, Patrick, testified to speaking with Jessie that early evening and said he witnessed her get into a white van and leave at approximately 5:30pm.

VONDA'S CAR
If Jessie borrowed Vonda's car, which she used to drive to her place in Cross Anchor, then what happened to Vonda's car when Jessie left in the white van? Did anyone question Patrick about whether or not he noticed Vonda's car was left behind or if it was ever there at all? If Vonda's car was not seen there at 5:30pm by Patrick, then what did Jessie do with Vonda's car and who dropped Jessie off at her own house? If Vonda's car was left behind at Jessie's place when she left in the white van, who returned it to Vonda's, and why?

BARE FEET

Let's take a moment to consider that when Jessie's body was found, she was barefoot and her shoes (to my knowledge) were never recovered. Where are you most likely to go barefoot? At home, right? So, if Jessie was barefoot at home at 5:30pm and left in a white van... did she not put on shoes or flip flops to leave? What sort of circumstance would cause you to leave your home barefoot? Perhaps Jessie didn't leave willingly. Perhaps she was coerced into the van against her will... shoes or no shoes.

VONDA'S CAR RETURNS

At around 6:00pm, Vonda noticed her car has been returned, but did not see who returned it. She saw a white van down in the road near her driveway, which left after the person who returned her car entered the van as a passenger.

VONDA LEAVES HER HOUSE

Vonda traveled from her house to Lillian's, who lives on Charles Humphreys Rd. Lillian testified to Vonda arriving at her house at 7:00pm. It takes approximately 35 minutes to travel from Vonda's house to Lillian's without traffic. We can assume Vonda left her house around 6:25pm. Keep in mind it was a Friday evening so we can assume Vonda probably did go through some traffic. Vonda took Jessie's youngest son with her to Lillian's, but Jessie's oldest son was napping when she left, so he stayed behind with Vonda's husband, Don.

LILLIAN'S TESTIMONY

When Vonda arrived at Lillian's, she was there to pick up Lillian's great granddaughter, who is close with Vonda's family, and for all intents and purposes is considered Vonda's granddaughter (but not biologically or through marriage). Lillian testified to walking the little girl out to Vonda's car and chatting with

Vonda before putting the young girl in the front passenger seat. Lillian testified to not seeing any blood in the vehicle at that time (7:00pm) and she did not notice any behaviors exhibited by Vonda that would be considered out of the ordinary.

JESSIE'S BODY IS FOUND

At approximately 7:30pm, a 9-1-1 call was made by a Jud Neal Loop resident who had been out for a walk with his dog when he discovered a body, later identified to be Jessie, down an embankment off a secluded stretch of Jud Neal Loop.

ESTIMATED TIME OF DEATH

To my knowledge and the knowledge of many others, including a young intern who was employed by the DA (District Attorney AKA the prosecution) at the time and whose desk Jessie's autopsy report allegedly landed on, there was no official estimated time of death included on the autopsy report and, therefore, we are missing absolutely vital information and must resort to theorizing. If Jessie was last seen at 5:30pm by Patrick and her body was discovered around 7:30pm, we have a 2-hour window to assume her death occurred. Where was Vonda between 5:30pm and 7:30pm? For starters, Vonda was at home with her husband and Jessie's two sons at 5:30pm and without her vehicle until approximately 6:00pm, when it was returned.

If Vonda arrived at Lillian's at 7:00pm, that would have given Vonda a 15-20 minute window to load Jessie's youngest son into her car, track Jessie down, kill her, dispose of her body, clean her car, change her clothes, clean herself up and then head to Lillian's. Not to mention the time it took to throw out Jessie's belongings along Betsy Ross Rd. Is Vonda a time traveler?

I think not. All these activities are not physically possible to commit within a 20-minute window.

Now we play devil's advocate and decide if and how Vonda could have murdered Jessie with our "Vonda DID do it" timeline and theory. We imagined that Vonda, Jessie and her sons left Food City at approximately 3:47pm. Could Vonda have killed Jessie after leaving Food City? The answer is no because Don has stated that Jessie did come over to their house after grocery shopping, which was around 4:10pm or shortly after. Some have speculated that Jessie never left Vonda's alive, but Jessie's neighbor spoke with her at her place just before 5:30pm. So... the only opportunity Vonda had to murder her was that 15-20 minute window after her car returned and before she arrived at Lillian's. This scenario sounds incredibly unlikely and physically impossible to me.

Now we'll theorize that a couple of details are lies and see how it could alter things. Let's say Vonda's husband LIED about the four of them returning to his and Vonda's home after grocery shopping. We know the groceries made it into Jessie's house because either John or one of her family members testified to seeing the grocery bags upon entering the house in their search for Jessie later that evening. So, they left Food City and unloaded the groceries... then what? If Don lied and the four were never at Vonda's together, then Vonda could have killed Jessie after the groceries were unloaded, right? Wrong. We still have Patrick, the neighbor, who spoke to Jessie at 5:30pm and watched her leave in the white van.

OK... so that theory pretending Don lied doesn't work.

Let's pretend Jessie's neighbor Patrick lied about speaking with Jessie and seeing her get into a white van. I can't fathom this witness to have a motive to lie, but hey, let's go for it. They leave Food City, drop off the groceries, go over to Vonda's house and then Jessie leaves in Vonda's car and isn't seen again until her body is found around 7:30pm. In this scenario, Vonda would also have to be lying about Jessie ever leaving her house at all. So, we'll pretend both Patrick and Vonda are lying. With this theory, Vonda would have had to murder Jessie outside her home, which is almost laughable. Did Vonda kill Jessie in her front yard and then go dispose of her body? How could she physically manage that? Wouldn't Don notice his wife murdering someone out front? Sorry sleuths... but this theory relies on some serious stretching of the imagination, and in order for this theory to work everyone would have to be lying. Additionally, it doesn't explain BOTH Patrick's and Vonda's separate accounts of seeing a white van, with only 30 minutes between each of their sightings of it.

We need to talk about the white van now. Jessie got into a white van, possibly against her will, at 5:30pm and assuming it's the same white van, it reappears at Vonda's 30 minutes later at around 6:00pm, when Vonda's car was returned. So where could the white van have traveled in that 30-minute span of time? Drum roll please....

White van leaves Jessie's place on Cross Anchor (with her inside) and travels up Baileyton Road, hangs a right onto Babbs Mill Road, gets to the intersection of where Babbs Mill Road meets Betsy Ross Road and Tyne Gray Road (Betsy Ross Road turns into Tyne Gray Road and what divides them is Babbs Mill Road) so the white van pauses at this intersection and chucks Jessie's cell phone out, which lands on a property to the right of Babbs Mill Road... on Tyne Gray Road (see upcoming map).

Perhaps Jessie was trying to call for help and they snatched her phone from her and tossed it out... where it would later be pinged, and its location determined to be right there, on Tyne Gray Road.

After the phone is tossed, the van turns left onto Betsy Ross Road, where some items belonging to Jessie are later found. The van crosses over Doty Chapel Road and travels up Jud Neal Loop, where Jessie was later found. After the white van disposes of her body, they continue to follow Jud Neal Loop out to Doty Chapel Road and onto Davis Valley Road. Vonda's car has been following the white van since it left Jessie's place... with an unknown driver. Perhaps an individual who arrived in the white van at Jessie's jumped in Vonda's car and followed behind... and THEY were the ones to throw Jessie's belongings out of Vonda's car. Both the white van and Vonda's car turn up at Vonda's house around 6:00pm. They left Jessie's at 5:30pm. The entire trip takes 24 minutes if you're not speeding. This theory fits like a glove, but there is one question that needs answering. Why wouldn't "they" have just left Vonda's car behind at Jessie's? If Vonda's car was actually at Jessie's to begin with, "they" might have thought that returning it would quell suspicion about Jessie's whereabouts and buy them time. Or maybe the intent was not to kill her, but something went wildly wrong and they panicked. Or... this was all premeditated and Vonda was the target of a set up the entire time, which is why Vonda's car was both returned and found to have blood inside.

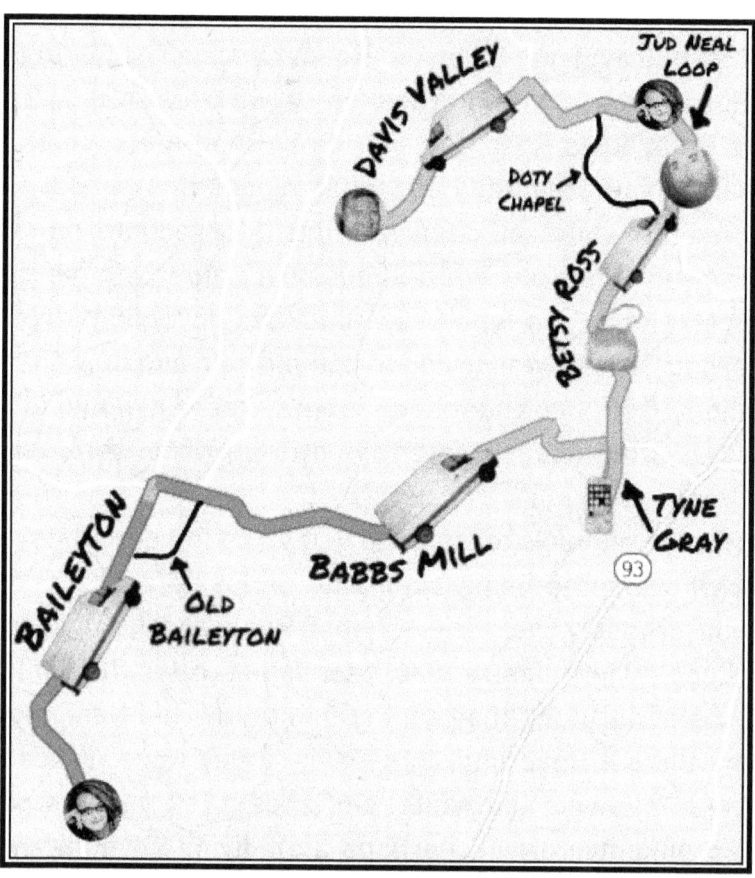

The map on the previous page illustrates the route for the theory we just went over. You'll notice Jessie's icon to indicate her home on Cross Anchor Park and a second icon to indicate where she came to be found on Jud Neal Loop. We speculate that Jessie got into the white van and was driven up Baileyton, then onto Babbs Mill, where a possible struggle might have been taking place inside the van at that point. Maybe Jessie was in the back of the van (think work-van-type) and a man or men in the back with her were assaulting her. Maybe Jessie had her cell phone and tried to dial 9-1-1, but it was snatched from her hand and thrown out of the passenger side window just as the van turned off Babbs Mill and onto Betsy Ross. If her cell phone was in fact thrown out of the window at this intersection, her phone would have flown in the direction of Tyne Gray Road, where our cell phone icon appears.

Shortly after Jessie's death, Detective Buddy Randolph had her cell phone pinged in hopes of retrieving its location and recovering the phone for clues and evidence. The phone ping was successful and, from what I've been told, Detective Randolph allegedly went to the location where the phone was pinged and that location turned out to be on Tyne Gray Road, not far at all from its intersection with Babbs Mill Road.

Rumor suggests that Detective Randolph never recovered the phone and when he questioned the residents at the house nearest to the ping location, the residents told him that they never saw a cell phone and didn't know anything about it. This cell phone ping information never made its way to Vonda's attorney, Steven, and he was left completely unaware it was ever performed. This evidence was withheld from the defense and Steven was rumored to have been upset that he wasn't informed about it and that he didn't have the chance to speak to the residents on Tyne Gray Road himself.

Once the white van turned onto Betsy Ross, maybe the unknown driver of Vonda's car, whom we speculate was following behind the van, was alerted to the struggle inside the van, and at that point, he or she began to frantically throw Jessie's belongings out of Vonda's car. The yellow purse icon indicates where a few items belonging to Jessie were found scattered along Betsy Ross including Manning's discharge paperwork from his oral surgery earlier that morning, a pair of children's shorts (presumably Manning's or Sam's) and some other papers. Keep in mind, we're speculating with this particular theory that these items found on Betsy Ross were thrown from Vonda's car, but there is no proof that these items were thrown from a vehicle at all.

Following Betsy Ross, we now speculate that the van crossed over Doty Chapel and drove up Jud Neal Loop. You'll notice Travis' icon on Jud Neal Loop because he was rumored to have been living there at the time of Jessie's death. Feel free to refer back to his player profile in Chapter Three for a refresher. Travis' alleged residency on Jud Neal Loop will come into play in our next theory.

Following Jud Neal Loop up and around, we come to Jessie's second icon, where we now speculate that her body was disposed of off the side of the road and partially down an embankment. From here, we imagine the white van, with Vonda's car still following behind, fled from the scene, where they crossed back over Doty Chapel and then drove down Davis Valley Road. Once on Davis Valley, Vonda's car was returned to her driveway and the unknown driver of her vehicle got into the white van, which was the white van Vonda claimed to have seen down in the road when she looked out her window and saw that her car had been returned.

This wraps up the timeline of our first theory of what could have happened to Jessie, but we're still left with questions that need answering. Who was in the van with Jessie? Who drove Vonda's car? What was their motive? Why did they return Vonda's car? Why were Jessie's belongings allegedly thrown out along

Betsy Ross Road? How did Jessie's blood get in Vonda's car? To help us better understand the gleaming wrench thrown into this theory, every other theory and into this entire case, we must discuss the blood in the car.

It has been rumored that most members of the jury convicted Vonda based solely on the fact that Jessie's blood was found in Vonda's car. But how did the blood get in there? This is the million-dollar question. A question not even the authorities or prosecution could offer an answer to.

Jessie's blood was found in Vonda's car, but when and by whom? Did Sheriff Hankins and his detectives, Buddy Randolph and Danny Ricker, find blood in Vonda's car when they searched it in the early morning following the murder? Was the blood the "stuff" they discovered in her car prior to sealing it as evidence and having it towed to TBI (Tennessee Bureau of Investigation)? If they did see blood in the car at that time, wouldn't they have arrested Vonda in that moment? If Jessie's body was discovered around 7:30pm and Lillian testified to NOT seeing any blood in Vonda's car at 7:00pm when Vonda arrived to pick Jemma up, but then the sheriff and detectives found blood in Vonda's car that Saturday morning around 2am, how did Jessie's blood get inside the car? We speculated that Vonda returned home from Lillian's in Limestone between 7:45pm and 8:00pm. Once Vonda returned home, she and her husband, Don, stayed inside their home with Manning, Sam and Jemma. Vonda's car remained parked in their driveway near the road until it was eventually towed to TBI several hours later.

The reality of the situation is that Vonda's car was left unattended from approximately 8:00pm to 2:00am the next morning. That leaves a six-hour window for anyone in East Tennessee to have access to Vonda's car because out here in the country it's not only customary to leave your vehicle unlocked, many also keep their keys inside their unlocked vehicle when at home, me included. There was one individual who did see the blood in Vonda's car. That individual was the tow truck driver, Troy. Troy once told a family member that when he had arrived to tow Vonda's car that morning, he attempted to open the vehicle to put it in neutral to make loading it easier, but his attempt was halted by either the sheriff or one of his detectives. Troy wasn't permitted to open the vehicle whatsoever, but he claims he saw a lot of blood in the car when he looked through the window. Unfortunately, Troy passed away unexpectedly in March 2018 so we cannot ask him about the blood he allegedly saw in the car. The amount of blood found in the car is also in question. Some individuals who attended the trial and were shown photos of the interior of the car say it was a small amount, only drops. Others claim that the amount of blood in the car was significant. I was once told that it was rumored that Vonda's attorney, Steven, allegedly removed or cut a small portion of the passenger seat's fabric, only for it to reveal that the blood in question never even penetrated the seat cushion, that the blood drops were so insignificant they remained on the fabric only.

I have seen a courtroom picture of the projector screen displaying the photo taken of the interior of Vonda's car and it is amazingly deceiving. What appears to be massive blood stains on the passenger seat also simply looks like a dirty seat. Vonda's car was a '94 or '95 model Pontiac and definitely had some wear and tear. Nothing against nothing, but I doubt she was in the business of maintaining a spotless car. Speaking of a clean car... let's talk about cat piss.

As luck would have it, the weekend prior to Jessie's death, Vonda was visiting her sister-in-law, Pam. Pam and Dale's front porch is lined with rocking chairs and this is where they and their company sit and chat and spend their afternoons and evenings. The porch looks out on the front lawn, which disappears beneath their gravel driveway. Most visitors drive up the gravel driveway and park just barely in the grass, leaving maybe a distance of

15-20 feet from the front of their parked vehicle to the porch. On the day Vonda was visiting Pam and Dale, this was the scenario.

It was an August afternoon and you know it was hot as balls outside. Vonda left her windows rolled down when she parked in Pam and Dale's yard. We all routinely leave our car windows rolled down during hot months because we don't want to suffocate in a scorching car when we are ready to leave. There became a problem with this strategy at Pam and Dale's house, however. They had cats. They had a shit ton of cats. What started out as maybe four cats quickly multiplied because none of them were spayed or neutered. Four cats turned into twelve cats and twelve cats turned into God only knows.

With so many cats, they certainly couldn't afford to spay and neuter them all! What's more, the cats lived in an old shed out back and weren't exactly domesticated. Dale fed them each day and made sure they had water but petting and snuggling the cats as beloved pets wasn't part of the relationship they had with their growing number of felines. The cats, therefore, were (and still are) feral. One such feral cat, that had not been spayed or neutered, jumped into Vonda's car through the open window. That was not the first time one of Pam and Dale's cats had jumped into a vehicle. I had a cat jump into my car on occasion as well. Pam had had cats jump inside her car, too.

Anyway, this feral cat jumped in Vonda's car that day and sprayed the seat. Neither of the women saw the cat jump inside the car, but they did witness it climbing out. When Vonda got back in her car to go home, she realized what had happened. We all know that odor and I think most of us can identify it immediately. It reeks. So Vonda called Pam and told her that the cat had sprayed the seat. She wanted to know what she could use to clean it and get the smell out. Pam wasn't sure what to use, so she suggested bleach. Vonda ultimately purchased a bottle of chemicals at the store and returned home to work on her pissy seat. Ordinarily, this entire situation would amount to nothing memorable at all, but when you clean your car seat with chemicals to get cat stank out of it and a few days later a dead girl's blood is found in your car, it tends to look suspicious. And that's exactly what happened.

When Vonda's car was towed to TBI and all the fancy forensic crap was done to it, the chemical Vonda had used to clean the cat piss up was dried into the fabric and possibly the cushioning of the seat. To find chemicals and blood together in a seat is a red flag for the forensic dudes and that sounded an alarm. Had Vonda tried to clean the blood out of her car? The answer is no, but the timing of it sure was spectacularly awful. So, there's that.

Now, my sleuths… crack another beer because I'm about to throw in a wild curve ball, which is going to lead us down a path we cannot come back from.

Lights a cigarette

Jessie's mother, Susan testified during the trial that she had had plans with her daughter the evening of Jessie's death. Susan wanted to visit with her grandsons. Presumably, this is what sparked Susan's concern about her daughter's whereabouts. She had plans to spend time with Jessie and the boys but could not get hold of Jessie and Jessie was not at her home.

I have an issue with Susan's testimony for several reasons. If we look back at Jessie's actions that day, there is nothing about her day that indicates she ever had plans with her mother. Let's consider the start of Jessie's morning. She took Manning to Johnson City for his oral surgery. Where was Susan? After Manning's surgery, Jessie went to Vonda for help, who was AT WORK. Where was Susan? Vonda took Jessie grocery shopping and then drove Jessie and her boys to Jessie's house with the groceries. If Jessie had plans with her mom that day or even that night, why didn't Jessie just stay at home with her boys at that point? After all, it was already approximately 4pm by the time they got to her house with the groceries. Jessie left her boys in the care of Vonda and Don at their house while she borrowed Vonda's car to go pay bills with the $1,000 cash Vonda had given her. Where was Susan?

According to a convoluted online article about Susan's trial testimony, Susan drove to Jessie's house to see if she was home. Not finding her daughter at home, Susan and her youngest daughter then drove to Vonda's house. They arrived at Vonda's sometime between 10:00pm and 11:00pm, which means they had been at Jessie's sometime between 9:45pm and 10:45pm. After her visit to Vonda's, Susan allegedly went back to Jessie's, where she and Jessie's boyfriend, John, searched the trailer for any unusual signs or clues as to where Jessie could be.

Now let's stop right here and consider some things. If Susan couldn't get hold of Jessie via texting or calling, did she ever contact John or Vonda before driving all the way to Jessie's place in Greeneville from her own home in Rogersville? Come to think of it, where was Susan that day? Did she work? If John was home by 7:30pm or so and came home to an empty house, did he attempt to text or call Jessie to see where she and the boys were? If he didn't try to get a hold of her, why? If he did try but was unsuccessful, did he call Vonda? Why does there seem to be no communication between Susan and John and Susan and Vonda and John and Vonda if Susan was so concerned about Jessie's whereabouts? What's more... I don't particularly believe Susan ever had plans with her daughter that day, so why the fuss about her whereabouts? Jessie was an adult and a mother and she could have easily been at the county fair that was in town that weekend. Jessie and Susan probably did not have a good relationship, and examining Jessie's relationship with Vonda proves that, in my opinion. Not only that, one of Jessie's sisters actually chewed out their mother about this in a public Facebook post made in September 2017, one year and one month after Jessie's death:

Morrison
Sep 20 at 10:31pm

I wish so much that I could've been there to take my sisters place. She didn't deserve any of this and still doesn't seem right. I question myself daily asking myself why those heartless people had to be so mean and do this. Even tho I can't be around the boys because my moms a piece of shit I know they suffer without their momma and don't understand what went wrong. I miss you Jessie more than anything and rather I'm there or not your boys will be taken care of. Maybe not how you wanted but we've all tried to prevent that. I love you and miss you so much.

11   5 Comments

Your mom tried to help you but you gotta help yourself also girl you got a child of your own so time to grow up

8 hours ago · Like · Reply

Morrison
I have grown up a hell of alot more than you have. A mom that cares doesn't tell her child to get out at one in the morning knowing I don't have a car but that's fine I had a ride so don't you worry about anything I do. Take your beer and shove it up your ass.

Note: "Frog" is a nickname they have for Manning.

I didn't tell you to get I said find somewhere to go cause your not gonna stand in my house and cuss me when all I ask you was where's Frog!

5 hours ago · Like · Reply

Morrison
Bullshit you bitched cause he stayed with dad. You ain't gonna keep him from his papaw. He loves his papaw and at least his damn papaw doesn't drink and drive with them. He's the one that said he didn't wanna stay there so he went with dad oh well. He stays with you all through the week two nights with dad doesn't hurt him. Actually better off for him

Morrison
You ain't been drinking my ass. You don't want dcs knowing shit but like you told uncle Sammy you quit drinking that was a lie. You was drinking the night you came in. I'll prove. I'll pay someone to catch your ass all they gotta do is show up around night time and that's all they'll smell is beer.

3 hours ago · Like · Reply

Morrison
You can't stand the fact frog would rather be with dad.

Go for it babe

3 hours ago · Like · Reply

Morrison
K stay off my shit. Me nor my kids have any reason to contact you. We aint shit to you

 **Morrison**
3 hrs

Wish someone would take this into consideration. Here mom when SAM needs diapers go without your beer and cigs instead of asking everyone else to buy them for you so you can keep drinking.

I've heard plenty of rumors about Susan and part of me wonders if she could possibly know what happened to her daughter that night. Aside from her alleged drinking, I've heard that she might have had dealings with more unsavory substances. I've also heard rumors that allege she might have friends in high places and that she and her special friends may or may not trade whatchamacallits for thingamajigs and vice versa. The rumor that really piques my interest though is the one that alleges Susan was actually at an old friend's house early that evening, just two miles from Jessie's house. This is all hearsay of course, but rumor has it that Susan showed up, out of the blue, at her friend's house on Old Baileyton around 5:00pm. Her friend and his wife had allegedly recently cut ties with Susan so they were somewhat surprised when she showed up unannounced.

Rumor also has it that Susan had allegedly been drinking that day and may or may not have been intoxicated by the time she arrived at her friend's house at 5:00pm. By 6:00pm, the rumor alleges that Susan began to freak out while at her friend's house, proclaiming that Jessie was missing and that she wanted to go file a police report. Susan's friends have allegedly stated that Susan's behavior that day was very odd indeed, and if this rumor has any possible truth to it, I would imagine this piece of information might be sensationally damning. Let's pretend this wild rumor is true. If Susan was at her friend's house just two miles down the road from Jessie's house around 5:00pm and was still there at 6:00pm, that means that Jessie either drove or was driven past that same road her mom was allegedly on (Old Baileyton) around 5:30pm when Jessie was unknowingly headed to her death. Looking at the map, Old Baileyton connects Baileyton to Babbs Mill. There is a possibility that the white van, with Jessie likely inside of it, could have even turned onto Old Baileyton to get to Babbs Mill, which would mean it drove directly past Susan while she was at her friends' house.

Still pretending this rumor could possibly be true so that I can indulge you all (and myself) in ridiculously fictitious theories and complete and total nonsense, let's consider the six o'clock hour. If Susan was at this friend's house and started talking crazy talk about Jessie being missing and her wanting to file a missing person report at 6:00pm, that was the same time Vonda's car was being returned to her driveway. More to the point, what caused Susan to think Jessie was missing or in danger that early on? Did she know something was going to happen to her daughter?

Let's continue to play pretend in my delusional world of theory and ask ourselves how Susan might have allegedly known that her daughter was in danger. What possible scenario could exist in which something bad was going to happen to Jessie and her mother knew about it? To answer that question, we need to consider Susan's rumored character and lifestyle. If, by chance, she was involved in illegal activities, she may or may not have also been involved with seedy people. What kind of people are typically involved in illegal activities? Criminals, drug addicts, drug dealers, drug runners, gangs and cartels. We have a mixed bag to choose from considering we're talking about East Tennessee, and Greene County in particular.

Let's pretend that Susan possibly had friends in low places and that these "friends" felt they were owed something in some capacity. Let's pretend Susan hadn't paid her dues and her "friends" became angry and wanted to collect. You've seen the movies, right? Gangs and cartels dealing drugs and then some asshole doesn't come through like they were supposed to and what happens? The gang or cartel sends a message. They always send a message. Maybe Jessie was the message.

Maybe Susan was warned about certain repercussions. Maybe the message wasn't intended for Susan at all. Maybe the message was intended for JT, who was a known drug dealer and who also lived with Jessie. Where was JT that day anyhow? He did testify during the trial that he and his buddy, Bradley, were at the trailer JT and Jessie both lived at on Cross Anchor that day and that they were driving his son Benjamin's white van. I wonder why they weren't driving Bradley's white van. In any event, JT and Bradley were in the trailer and per JT's testimony, they were there around 3:45pm. JT went on to say that they saw the groceries on the kitchen floor, but that's not possible because, at that time, Jessie and Vonda had barely even left Food City, let alone dropped the groceries off yet.

This is where all the complicated shit gets more complicated. This is where my mom and I started going down various rabbit holes. The more questions we searched for answers to, the more questions we ended up with. If Jessie's death was drug related, who in her circle could be allegedly involved with drugs? Well, as it turns out, that question was not so easy to answer. By a stroke of luck, however, an old friend of Greene County stopped by my house one summer night in 2018 with a cooler full of cold beer and a very intriguing story of his own.

My friend, we'll call him Buck. Buck's a good 'ol boy if you ever met one. He's in his fifties and has lived in Greene County his entire life. Sure, he's had brushes with the law for drunkenness, but he's good people nonetheless. He got out of his pickup truck and sauntered over to us in our front yard with a beer in hand. We only see Buck a couple times a year, so it's a treat when he stops by. We all sat in lawn chairs out front as the sun was going down, drinking beer and catching up. The conversation somehow turned to Vonda and my work on the case. We talked about Jessie and the night she was murdered. Jud Neal Loop was mentioned and that's when the conversation took an unexpected turn.

Buck lit a cigarette and told us that when he had heard about the murder on Jud Neal Loop, he instantly thought that a pair of siblings he once knew had something to do with it. He went on to tell us that those siblings once lived under his roof. Years back, he had dated their mother and the four of them had all lived together. Buck worked long hours and when he returned home at the end of the day, his girlfriend and her kids were very attentive to him. His girlfriend always had supper on the table with a glass of sweet tea for him. After finishing his meal, Buck would usually go straight to bed. He told us that he was just so tired after working so hard and after eating a good meal that he would quite literally pass out. Weeks went by this way and, as they did, Buck became ill.

Being a tough, country boy, Buck just dealt with his ailments. He was getting frequent headaches and having stomach pains. As his symptoms progressed, his headaches turned into migraines and his stomach pain was causing him to vomit blood. At this point, he said, is when he finally dragged his ass to the emergency room. Doctors did some routine bloodwork to see what was going on and the results weren't anything anyone was expecting.

Buck told us the doctor came in the room and told him that he had arsenic and antifreeze in his blood, and he had enough of it in him to kill a horse. The doctor had no idea how Buck was still alive. Obviously, someone was poisoning him. Buck took a day or two to figure out what was going on. He ultimately decided it was the sweet tea he was being served with his supper. He told us that his girlfriend and her kids never drank the sweet tea at the house... that he had his own special pitcher of it in the fridge.

I was on the edge of my lawn chair listening to Buck's story and could barely believe that was the reason for his current stomach issues. Of course, I pressed him about what he did after he realized his girlfriend and possibly her kids were trying to kill him! He said he just left. He knew how the county worked, so he just up and left. He went on to say that his ex-girlfriend and her kids moved into a house on Jud Neal Loop (the address will remain anonymous). Evidently, the woman's grown children were still living in that same house at the time of Jessie's death.

Amazingly enough, I had gotten a phone call from another friend that same day, just an hour or so before Buck stopped by. This friend, whom we'll call Jimmy, lives very near Jud Neal Loop and can see any traffic coming and going at the end of the loop closest to Betsy Ross Road. Jimmy called to tell me he had a sneaking suspicion that there was a drug house on Jud Neal Loop. The address he gave me was the same address Buck was now telling us his ex-girlfriend and kids had moved to. I could not fucking believe it! My mom and I went batshit. This alleged drug house on Jud Neal Loop spawned a new investigation.

Chapter Five

In the days following our newest leads, my mom snooped around Facebook until she found a guy named Travis. It appeared as though this guy was one of the siblings Buck had known years ago. It also appeared that Travis had been living at the house in question on Jud Neal Loop for several years and was likely living there at the time of Jessie's death. As for Travis' sister, we discovered she was very pregnant at the time of Jessie's death and had given birth shortly after, so we ruled her out as a player of any sort.

Travis, on the other hand, we were very interested in. Judging by his public Facebook profile and photos, it seemed as though he might have partaken in extracurricular activities. It was apparent he belonged to the LGBTQ community and identified as such, so we concluded he was likely not one of Jessie's attackers, but his hobbies and location won him a spot on our growing player list.

Further research revealed more intrigue. I discovered that just a month or so after Jessie's death Travis up and left for Texas. From what I could tell, he wasn't there on vacation because he had gotten himself a j-o-b. Interestingly, Jessie's ex-boyfriend and father to her youngest son, Shane, also lived in Texas. Remember that guy? Travis was now living in the same city in the second largest state in America as Jessie's ex. What an amazing coincidence!

Based on my snooping and in my own personal opinion, I got the impression that Travis might have really been struggling emotionally during the period of time following Jessie's death. It also kind of looked as though he dialed up his extracurricular activities a notch. I guessed that something was bothering him. A couple of months after landing in Texas, Travis came back to Tennessee, but it appeared that he no longer lived on Jud Neal Loop. He resurfaced in the Tri-Cities of Northeast Tennessee.

Travis' friends list on Facebook, which has since been set to private, included nearly every person on our player list, plus some. OK, so this guy knows a bunch of alleged drug addicts and alleged drug dealers… that doesn't make him a murderer, but it could make his old house on Jud Neal Loop a fantastic hangout for like-minded people.

I bet Bradley and Benjamin could be like-minded people. In fact, Travis was Facebook friends with them both. Benjamin even appears to be a member of the LGBTQ community as well. They just seem to have so much in common, like two peas in a pod. Maybe Benjamin and Bradley and Travis are all friends or acquaintances in real life. Maybe we found ourselves a new theory.…

What if Jessie didn't get into the white van? What if her neighbor was confused about what he had witnessed or even possibly lied in his testimony? What if it was JT, Bradley, and Benjamin in the white van and they had come back to the trailer while Jessie was there. Maybe they asked her if she wanted to go hang out at Travis' house or go to the county fair. Maybe Jessie did want to hang out with them because, after all, Benjamin was a close friend and JT was her boyfriend's father. They were like family. So, rather than Jessie getting into the white van as Patrick had testified, maybe Jessie got into Vonda's car and told the guys that she needed to return it, so they'd have to follow her. Maybe Jessie returned Vonda's car because she knew Vonda had plans to drive to Limestone that evening to pick up Jemma. The following map depicts what it might look like if Jessie returned Vonda's car herself.

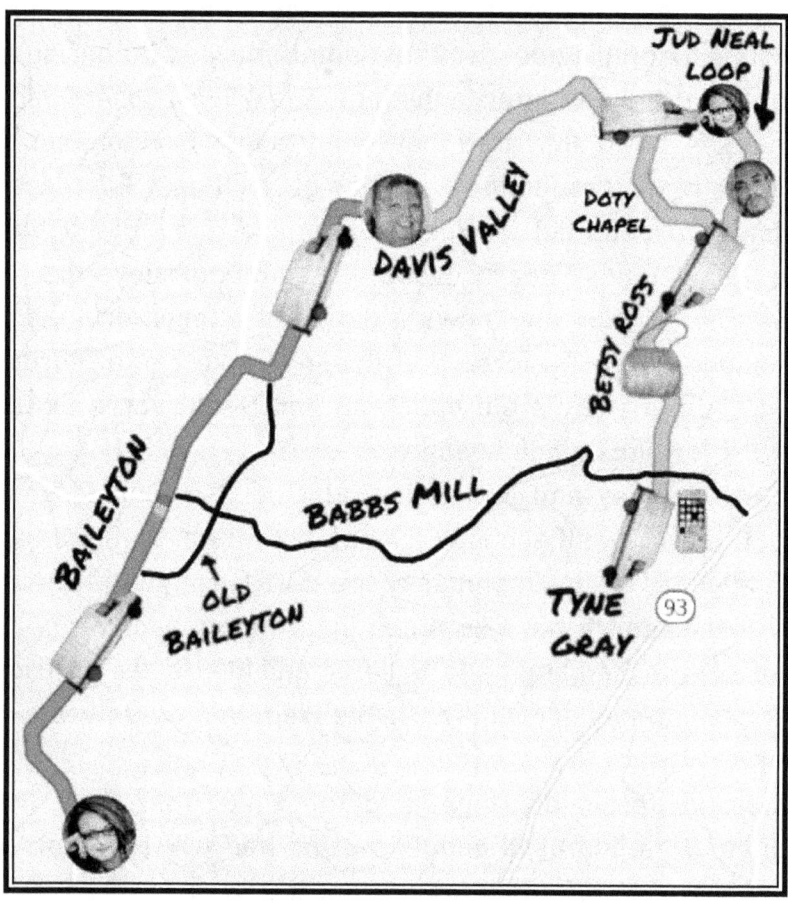

With this theory, Jessie returned Vonda's car herself and then got into the white van with JT, Bradley, and Benjamin. Jessie didn't alert Vonda that she'd returned the car because, let's face it guys, her two young sons were inside and what happens when little ones see their parent? Jessie was probably just pulling a mom sneaky-sneak by quietly returning the car. Now let's pretend the four of them drove over to Travis' house on Jud Neal

Loop just a couple of miles away. If Travis' house was a possible hub for hobbies, then there might have been a few people at the house. It was a Friday evening after all.

So let's say the four of them went and hung out at Travis' and, being pregnant, Jessie wants to kick her feet up while they're hanging out. Maybe she was on a couch or on a bed and took her flip flops off before putting her feet up. Maybe JT and Bradley or some other men who might have been there hanging out decided to get high. Maybe they started to tease Jessie and it went too far. Maybe Jessie was raped or nearly raped, and in her fury and possibly out of fear, she stormed out of the house barefoot, leaving her flip flops behind.

If Jessie did storm out or run out of that house, she went up the loop rather than back toward the main road, Doty Chapel. Why would she go further around the loop? My guess is that she wanted some privacy after being attacked, and if there's one thing Jud Neal Loop offers, it's privacy. I think it's fairly reasonable to believe Jessie was making her way to Vonda's… to safety. But Jessie never made it to safety. Possibly high and probably panicked, the men who attacked Jessie decided to go after her in the white van. Maybe they caught up to her a short distance into her walk (or run) away from the house and forced her into the van, where things went wrong quickly and her body was disposed of further around the loop. On the other hand, maybe the white van caught up to her at the very location her final resting place would be. Maybe there was a struggle right there in the road and maybe Jessie fought back harder than they expected and maybe someone grabbed a metal object from inside the van and hit her in the back of the head with it to get her to stop fighting her attackers.

This theory seems to be a decent one, but how did Jessie's belongings get scattered on Betsy Ross Road and, once again, how and when did her blood get inside Vonda's car? Every damn time my mom and I think we might have nailed down a solid theory, we're still always left with one or two missing details, and we're most certainly always left with our gleaming wrench, the blood.

A couple of weeks after hammering out our second theory, a possible third theory emerged. My friend, Jimmy, called again and this time we talked at length about Jessie's murder. But that wasn't the only horror we discussed that day.

In the summer of 2017, a man named Lee knocked on his neighbor's door late one night. His friend, whom we'll call Alice, answered the door. Lee shot her in the leg with a shotgun and dragged her into her bedroom. He assaulted her and held her captive there for hours. Bleeding profusely and drifting in and out of consciousness, Alice refused to die... she was a mother and had to live for her children. Finally, Lee left and returned to his house, where his brother was also living. Lee told his brother that Alice was in trouble. Without any details other than knowing Alice was in trouble, Lee's brother ran over to her house, but was afraid to go inside because he didn't know if danger awaited him. Instead, he called 9-1-1. Police quickly went to Lee's house to question him. Lee allegedly confessed on the spot to what he had done and was arrested.

Alice is Jimmy's girlfriend. Jimmy told me that Lee, who lived on Jud Neal Loop at the time, had made a cross the day following Jessie's murder. Jimmy said it struck him as odd because, to his knowledge, Lee didn't know Jessie. A few days later, Lee had come over to drink some beers with Jimmy, and there having been a murder right down the road, Jimmy brought it up in conversation, but Lee refused to talk about it and kind of shut the conversation down.

Jimmy pressed Lee a bit more and all he could get out of him was a very peculiar comment. Lee told Jimmy that "they" (law enforcement) knew who did it and that it was the grandma. Lee was referring to Vonda, but how did law enforcement know it was Vonda just days after the murder and how did Lee know that they knew?

Jimmy went on to tell me that sometime just before Christmas of 2016 (four months after Jessie's death), he was talking to Lee and had mentioned that he was wanting to buy a van for work. A couple of days after that conversation, Jimmy ended up buying himself a van just as he wanted. When he got home with it, there was Lee… with a van for Jimmy. It was a white van and, by the looks of the inside, it appeared to have potentially stolen items in the back of it. He said that the van stayed parked on Lee's property for months and never moved until one day it was gone. Jimmy speculated that the white van Lee tried to give him had once belonged to Lee's friend, Bradley. Jimmy knew Bradley from elementary school. He had seen Bradley over at Lee's house on multiple occasions over the years. My mom and I both wondered if Bradley had dumped the white van on Lee to get rid of it. Not the brightest plan if it was the white van in question because it ended up right back on Jud Neal Loop on Lee's property. Maybe Bradley was going for that whole "hidden in plain sight" trick.

After Jimmy told me all about Lee's strange behavior regarding Jessie's murder and about the white van, he told me Alice's story. Jimmy said that after Alice had gone through surgery and came home from the hospital and recovered a bit (physically and emotionally), she told him that throughout the entire ordeal she had a strange feeling that Lee had possibly committed an act like that before. Alice said that despite what he was doing, Lee remained very calm the entire time. Alice was so convinced that her being attacked and assaulted by Lee wasn't his first rodeo that she went to the Greene County Sheriff's Department to express her concern and personal thoughts about Lee possibly being the one who killed Jessie, just 10 months prior to him attacking Alice.

Upon entering the department, Alice allegedly found law enforcement individuals so engrossed in television that they initially ignored her. She stood her ground and continued to press the matter. These law enforcement individuals allegedly brushed her off and stated that they got their suspect and that it was undeniably Vonda. Alice left the department feeling ignored as a victim, disrespected and defeated. To my knowledge, the Greene County Sheriff's Department has never questioned or even considered Lee to be a suspect in Jessie's murder. Adding insult to injury, Judge Dugger (the same judge who presided over Vonda's case) continues to reschedule Lee's trial, pushing it farther and farther out. Lee was arrested sometime in July 2017 when he confessed to his crime, but here we are two years later and he's still sitting in the county jail awaiting trial.

Greene County might not have an interest in Lee as a possible suspect in Jessie's murder, but the big dogs sure seem to:

Lee Allen Britton   Defendant   Jury Trial   09/24/2019 9:00 AM   John F Dugger Jr.

Lee Allen Britton   Defendant Announce Trail / MFC   09/03/2019 1:05 PM   John F Dugger Jr.

Lee Allen Britton	Defendant	Jury Trial	05/14/2019 9:00 AM	John F Dugger Jr.	Case Rescheduled

Lee Allen Britton	Defendant	Announcement trial/mfc	05/01/2019 1:05 PM	John F Dugger Jr.	Case Rescheduled

Lee Allen Britton	Defendant	Jury Trial	01/22/2019 9:00 AM	John F Dugger Jr.	Case Rescheduled

Lee Allen Britton	Defendant	Announcement trial/mfc	01/03/2019 1:05 PM	John F Dugger Jr.	Case Rescheduled

Lee Allen Britton	Defendant	Announcement trial/mfc	01/03/2019 1:00 PM	John F Dugger Jr.	Case Rescheduled

Lee Allen Britton   Defendant
Arraignment   07/31/2018
8:30 AM   John F Dugger Jr.   Case Rescheduled

Lee Allen Britton   Defendant
Arraignment   05/11/2018
8:30 AM   John F Dugger Jr.   Case Rescheduled

Lee Allen Britton   Defendant
Arraignment   03/29/2018
8:30 AM   John F Dugger Jr.   Case Rescheduled

Lee Allen Britton   Defendant
Arraignment   01/12/2018
8:30 AM   John F Dugger Jr.   Case Rescheduled

Lee Allen Britton   Defendant
Arraignment   11/30/2017
8:30 AM   John F Dugger Jr.   Case Rescheduled

Go ahead and crack another cold beer, sleuths, or grab a cup of coffee. Allow me to introduce you to "the big dogs."
   Lights a cigarette
   Sometime in late summer of 2018, a few months after Vonda's trial, I had Googled "top true crime producers" and my search revealed exactly that. My hope was to get more publicity for the

case and for Vonda's wrongful conviction. To do that, I reasoned, we needed someone who would be interested enough in the case to make a show or documentary about it.

I clicked on Joe Berlinger's profile. At the time, I had no idea who he was or what he produced, but after skimming his profile I decided I would e-mail him. I don't recall exactly what my e-mail entailed, but I must have mentioned the most important highlights of Vonda's case. Several weeks went by and by that time I was so involved in working on the case and e-mailing others who might help that I had nearly forgotten I'd e-mailed Mr. Berlinger. But then an e-mail came, and it was from one of his producers.

"Tessa" introduced herself as a producer at Radical Media in NYC. She said they were interested in Vonda's case and wanted to possibly feature it on their show, Wrong Man, which is on the Starz network. My first thought was "holy shit" and my second thought was "Oh my God, we're saved!" My mom and I were absolutely ecstatic!

After e-mailing back and forth a couple of times, Tessa asked if we could do a conference call with her and her colleague, "Caitlyn," who is also a producer at Radical Media. The day arrived, and they called just as they said they would. Our conversation centered around the same highlights of the case I'd initially e-mailed to Mr. Berlinger. The two women asked some additional questions about the case and, at the close of our conversation, asked me to e-mail them all the information I had and told me to keep in touch.

Cracks knuckles, blows on fingertips

Well... where to begin? Type, type, type, clickity-clack, type, type, type. I spent the next several weeks e-mailing the people I came to refer to as "the producers" everything my mom and I knew, everything we thought, everything we found. I e-mailed them facts about the case, personal theories my mom and I had formed, rumors I had heard... absolutely everything. Then one cold evening in February 2019, I finally met Caitlyn and her assistant, "Abby," for dinner. Caitlyn had come to Greeneville with her team, which included a camera crew. Also attending our dinner was an investigator from Nashville named "Maggie," who had been brought on board by the producers as their person on the ground here locally.

I was thrilled to be meeting them and was a little nervous, too. Small talk was brief because we were there for business. As we went over the case, they asked me a lot of questions. All three women busily took notes. At one point, I had mentioned something of such interest that Caitlyn grabbed her phone to relay the information to a team member back in NYC.

We discussed possible suspects, possible motives, and I told them about the rumors I'd been hearing about the whole mess being a potential cover-up. I offered them my perception of the county and my personal opinions about certain players, and explained the situation about the cat piss in Vonda's car in greater detail. All three women were so kind and gracious, and I could see that they were going to do their best to help us... to help Vonda. I hugged them all goodbye and we parted ways.

As my relationship with the producers was forming, I was still maintaining my blog on Tumblr and my mom and I were steady in the background, snooping and researching. During this time, my mom found an old Facebook post made by John's wife, Christy, prior to them getting married. I took a screen shot of that post and posted it to my Tumblr blog and mused over what it could mean. Here is that post:

Christy writes, "Its good to know even when hes thousands of miles away, he still puts in the effort to let me know he cares! Thank you [John], theyre beautiful! Merry Christmas to me."

My post about this is as follows:

Here we have a photo that JOHN'S now wife, CHRISTY posted to FB back on December 24, 2016.

Jessie Morrison, JOHN'S fiance at the time, was murdered August 12, 2016 and FOUR MONTHS later... JOHN is sending flowers to another girl???

Was he secretly dating CHRISTY at the time of Jessie's death? Did JOHN realize he wanted to only be with CHRISTY and felt that his pregnant fiance, Jessie, was in the way of his happiness? Could his wanting to only be with CHRISTY have been motive enough to kill Jessie? You decide.

14 notes

Now, what followed my post about John sending Christy flowers just four months after his alleged fiancée, Jessie, and his alleged unborn baby were MURDERED was an exchange I never saw coming. But before we get into what happened after I made that post I need to tell you what happened just last night (July 13th, 2019).

Last night I had just sat down to work on this book and was ready to introduce Christy. I decided I'd get on Tumblr and copy and paste a couple of my posts to use them here, in this book, which we'll get to in just a moment. When I found the post I was looking for, Post #39, which is what you've just viewed, I clicked on the comments for my post.

You can see in the screen shot that there are 14 "notes" on that particular post. These notes are the comments other users have left or some I have written myself. Well, after I had originally posted this on Tumblr, Christy appeared and left a very lengthy "note" on my post. When I clicked on the notes last night to reread her comment, it was gone. What's the big deal, you ask? The big deal is that it's a well-known fact that as a Tumblr user, once you comment on a post, your comment is there forever. There is no way to edit or delete your comment. Tumblr simply does not currently offer this particular feature, much to the frustration of its users. Many Tumblr users have taken to the internet to complain about this feature (or lack thereof) and, as far as I can tell, deleting a comment can't be done.

I texted my publisher, Steven Booth of Genius Publishing, to come to the rescue in hopes that he or one of his friends, being more tech savvy than myself and maybe more familiar with Tumblr, might know a way to delete a comment on Tumblr. If there isn't, how did Christy's comment on my post get deleted, who made it disappear, and why? What in the actual hell was going on? Sleuths, if there's one thing you gotta understand, it's that this case is still happening. As I write this book, at this very moment, Vonda is in prison, my mom and I are still working on the case, the producers are still working on the case and shit is still unfolding. There have been no fat ladies singing, no curtains have been drawn, this is still very much a live show, so to speak.

As it turns out, despite what Tumblr's help desk or whatever has to say, a comment made on a Tumblr post cannot be deleted.

With this new information, I really have no idea what to think. How was Christy's comment deleted? The only thing I can do now is use my active imagination and speculate.

First of all, I'm feeling fucking sweaty. If ordinary Tumblr users don't have the power to edit or delete their own comments, then who does have the power? Tumblr? Why would Tumblr randomly delete this chick's comment on my post? They wouldn't... because that doesn't make sense. Christy's comment could be viewed as unintentionally damning toward John, so the reason for it being deleted must mean someone doesn't want that information out there and that someone is trying like hell to protect John.

Let's think about this. Who wants to protect John and has the power to get a comment deleted from a site like Tumblr? My guess is an agency. Surely to God, Greene County Sheriff's Department doesn't have that kind of pull. Maybe TBI? FBI? CIA? I have no freaking clue, but I'm not feeling any less sweaty the more I think about it.

So there ya have it... that is what's happening right now as I write this book and it's a little window into what I'm going through. There is some messed up shit going on and it seems like it just keeps coming. There are some people out there that make fun of me and call me paranoid and laugh, but my gut tells me that I should be.

OK, I gotta move on with my story here, but if anything else arises between now and when I submit this manuscript to my publisher, I'll just throw it in because, like I said, I am writing this live as it happens.

Back to the ranch, sleuths. Christy's lengthy comment on my Tumblr post has been deleted, yes, but my mom is a badass and had taken screen shots of the whole shebang. My mom has taken screen shots of everything and she deserves a major award, like a glowing leg lamp for her window. Without further ado, the infamous and now missing comment:

I suggest if you are going to look through my facebook or my husband's, you don't knit pick what is useful for you while leaving out other information. 1. I had been dating the same boy for ten years. Well call him "Danny". we broke up a week before Christmas on top of my parents divorcing and I was having health problems. So him and his sister did something nice to cheer me up since I was alone for the holidays. **JOHN** sent me flowers and his sister came down to visit me. Nothing suspicious or wrong with that, especially considering I have been friends with the entire   family since I was a child. 2. Before Jessie and almost a year after Jessie, he had other relationships, some serious some not. None of the relationships involved me, you know, since I was still dating Danny. 3. They were never engaged. Not that it matters but that clearly shows your lack of knowledge. 4. We moved to Florida for closer and better healthcare for myself and our child. And finally, 5. No person would kill another person, especially a woman pregnant with his child, in an effort to get out of the relationship. Had he wanted out, he could have easily left her, he had no obligation to stay. Example A: he left the mother of his first child, and began dating jessie not long after. She's alive and well. So you tell me what difference is there between the two women? I suggest, A: you look at who Vonda could possibly be trying to cover for. My guess is someone in her family, someone she cares deeply for. B: begin looking for the unknown male who's semen was found in her in the autopsy.

And PS: if you are trying to prove Vonda's innocence, pointing fingers at everyone because of their past or making up ridiculous theories as to why someone would do it, without accounting for the evidence that is in hand makes everything you say seem flaky at best. Look at all of the evidence they have(ie: blood, camera footage, verifiable eye witnesses, yata yata), look at the time frame, look at who had time to do it, who had verifiable alibis, who was last seen with her(and can prove it), and what logical reason they could have had to do it. Not these crazy fantasized theories you are making that are far fetched as well as ridiculous. I personally believe she(Vonda) is covering for someone she cares about, because what other reason would she have to go on trial, be convicted, then say in prison that she knows who did it and will be telling the real story at her appeal, because she feels her efforts went unappreciated?.

Source: thealiensknow

I continue in Post #40...

Post #40

@CHRISTY

Welcome to Tumblr.

Your comment on Post #39 began with suggesting I not knit pick what is and what is not useful information. My team and I have gone through a variety of peoples' Facebook profiles and posts and we do "knit pick" everything before agreeing on what information might be useful and in turn, writing about various theories... knit picking is kind of the name of the game.

I will address your numbered points using the same method for easy following...

1. The flowers you received from JOHN ... you remarked in your December 24th 2016 post, that he was "thousands of miles away" at the time. The distance between east TN and the furthest most part of FL does not exceed 900 miles. So was JOHN out of state when he sent them?

2. Concerning JOHN's relationships prior to and following Jessie Morrison's death, it appears (in the Greeneville Sun as a matter

of fact) that he might have been in a relationship in July 2017 that resulted in an unknown female having her skull fractured. Do you have any comment on this?

3. You say that JOHN and Jessie Morrison were never engaged. Why does Jessie's obituary name JOHN as her fiance at her time of death?

4. Your relocation to FL occured in February or March of 2018 correct? Is it true that sometime in February 2018 you posted to your Facebook that you

were going to FL alone and that you were facing, at that time, potentially being a future single parent? It appears you had a change of heart because you and JOHN were married later in February 2018. Congratulations, by the way. It does seem that the relocation to FL was a bit of a family affair... did JOHN's brother, BENJAMIN tag along for better health care, too?

5. A quick Google search will reveal that there have been countless murders committed by men who wanted out of relationships or for various other reasons. Let's not discount the

motivation of wanting "out". In fact, to broaden our horizons on this particular topic, I have provided a link below that you might find informative.

https://www.theatlantic.com/health/archive/2017/07/homicides-women/534306/

You'll have to manually type in the link in your search engine because an active link in this post would be misleading, as the link would include a photo and the topic of the link is not the purpose of this post.

Additionally, you stated that JOHN had no obligation to remain in a relationship with a pregnant Jessie Morrison, nor did he have any obligation to stay in a relationship with his other two children's mothers. To this I say, there is a very fine line, mostly a moral one, that suggests being a father is an obligation. I wonder... if JOHN were to leave you and your child high and dry some day, would you still hold the same opinion regarding parental obligation?

Regarding the possibility that Vonda is covering for someone... I ask this... if Vonda IS covering for someone, why then is there a rumor that JOHN allegedly hunted Vonda down, violently assaulted her, threatened at least her and her grandson, and then left her for dead?

and PS: Proving someone's innocence does mean pointing the finger away from them and in the direction of others. For example, in proving JOHN 's innocence, fingers were pointed at Vonda Smith. Moreover, none of the physical evidence proves beyond a reasonable doubt that Vonda Smith committed this crime. An ignorant jury, without all of the facts, sent her to prison on circumstantial evidence and a fabricated motive. You want to talk about "crazy fantasized theories"... let's start with the one about how Vonda Smith murdered Jessie Morrison.

Lastly, no one knows what Vonda knows or what HER story is. It's true that she should have spoken up in the beginning and probably should have taken the stand in her own defense... but when a person is hunted, violently attacked, threatened, and the safety of family members is at risk... one tends to keep one's mouth shut.

My team and I have been working diligently on this story in hopes of shedding some light on what really happened with this case. May I suggest you read this blog in its entirety and perhaps you'll then understand our perspective and means of gathering information and theorizing in hopes of securing justice for Vonda Smith and Jessie Morrison. Feel free to join the cause.

@CHRISTY Part II

Below is CHRISTY's reply to Post #40

OK 1. I put a thousand miles away, but was it accurate? No. Both he and I had jobs at the moment, so I assure you we were both in the town we resided in.

2. If you kept track of the skull fracture case, you would know it was thrown out and he was never charged. It was talked about in court and was nothing more than a domestic dispute. And to clarify, yes that was me. Since I'm sure everyone wonders. He didn't use excessive force. I'm on extensive

amounts of steroids, which in turn cause brittle bones. He slung me away from the door when I attempted to leave while drinking. I over reacted and took things out of context, but physically violent? No he never once physically hit/beat me. Slinging someone to the floor is completely and utterly different than continuously beating someone. And yes, we began dating late April. Before I moved to Tennessee, he was in a relationship with another woman.

3. I don't know why it says they were engaged, but for as much snooping as you've done, I'm sure at least once you would have came across some kind of post stating they were engaged. She never had a ring, was never given a ring, and was never proposed to. Meaning they were not engaged. Beyond that, I'm a part of the family, and have been told and heard numerous times from him and others they were not engaged. Personally, I don't see what it matters, but just saying, if we're gonna speak of facts, that is a fact.

4. At the time JOHN and I were arguing

a lot, maybe because of the stress of knowing the meds I had been taking, celcept, meant I had a 50/50 chance of losing the baby in the first trimester. That alone can put a couple through a lot of stress, especially when a woman has been told before that there's a possibility she could not have children. But we worked through our issues, moved like planned, and I began seeing the Dr who has provided my transplant healthcare since I was a teenager.
And NO, BENJAMIN didn't come to Florida. He is still in Tennessee. I'm a little confused as to why you think he tagged along?

5. I firmly stand by my comment. He did not have any obligation to stay. His only obligation is to his child/children. Say he does leave me in the future, I expect nothing from him. The only expectation I have from him is to continue being in his child's life. And as you can tell, once Jessie ends a relationship with someone, she no longer pursues them to fulfil their duty as a father. So do I think it would have been easy to leave? Yes. She was 21 years old, she had a family to support her and care for her had JOHN ever left her. But just saying, if you are going to suggest he killed her for a way out, to look at his pattern before Jessie.

Chances are, had he wanted out he would have repeated the same pattern and just left her like he did with the first mother of his child.

6. A rumor is just that. There was no evidence and at the time, JOHN did not own a vehicle. He was not even in town. Once again, all verified by tbi. So her story was fabricated or perhaps she was in such disarray her mind was boggled and she was just simply incorrect about what she thought happened. And to top that, them boys love JOHN. Her family loves JOHN. He has stayed actively involved in their life. It's quite silly to think if he had

murdered Jessie, (taking out of account the fact that he had a verifiable alibi, had a verifiable timeline, had eye witnesses, and had video footage to prove his timeline), that he would only assault Vonda and threaten her, not just kill her. And to keep family safe, I would not keep my mouth shut. I would, as would any normal person, do anything and everything in my power to make sure that person who did me harm and threatened my child or grandchild was found and locked up. I'd feel safer knowing they were off the streets. But regardless he was not in town at the time Vonda claims she was assaulted, which is partly why he was never charged along with many other reasons.

And as I stated before and I still believe and have even told my husband, given the things I've seen/heard/know about the case, I agree, Vonda was convicted for something I don't believe she personally did herself. I do believe she knows who did it, I believe she was involved, if nothing more, just by cleaning the blood out of the car and keeping the children, but I firmly believe she is covering for a family member of hers. Because if she cares that deeply about her grandchildren,

I can only imagine how much deeper her love for her immediate family is. Perhaps she knows who the third semen sample belongs to? Maybe Jessie was with someone she was keeping hidden, and maybe Vonda knew who that person was. Maybe a man Vonda was close with made advances towards Jessie and she stood her ground and said no, possibly making said man angry, and he took it too far and ended up killing her? There's a lot of theories, and I think there's a lot to the story of that day that Vonda knows but did not tell, but one thing is for sure,

JOHN did not do it, he was investigated thoroughly and everything he said matched the evidence they gathered to prove his whereabouts the entire day.

I enjoy keeping track of the work you have been doing, it's interesting to see different points of view and different theories, but quite a few of them you base off of bad foundations, such as petty theft charges, drug charges, old and new relationships, (and BTW: NICOLE, who you mentioned before that said she warned Jessie of JOHN's violent tendencies, brought her son to live with us for a few months after JOHN drove out of his way to pick them both up when she called him while her current boyfriend was beating her. No sane woman would leave her child in the care of someone she truly thinks murdered someone. Regardless of what she said and did in the past, he still tried to help her and her son. That speaks volumes of his character). I'm perfectly content answering any questions you may have, but I do not think you are going to get far by focusing on someone who has already been cleared.

My reply to this is as follows...

1. Skull Fracture Incident

You claim that your skull fracture was the result of a "domestic dispute". According to Dictionary.com, 'dispute' is a verb and means "to engage in argument or debate", both of which are verbal, non-physical. Dictionary.com defines 'violence' as "swift and intense force", "rough or injurious physical force, action, or treatment". With that said, it sounds like what you experienced, dear girl, was more likely domestic violence... so let's call a spade, a spade.

You mention you were on "extensive amounts of steroids" at the time of this incident and that they cause brittle bones. Based on the research my team and I have done, osteoporosis is the medical term for brittle bones. It appears that pro-longed use of steroids can cause osteoporosis, but scientific research suggests that differences between skull and limb bone are significantly profound. In a nutshell, skull bone is resistant to osteoporosis.

An informative article can be found here:

https://www.medicalnewstoday.com/articles/174621.php

I'm no medical expert, but it sounds as though your skull fracture was probably the result of force, not "brittle bones".

You also stated that you were "slung" away from the front door to prevent you from leaving while drinking. If this is true, one would have to assume that you had been consuming alcohol in excess to warrant such a physical response from an individual to prevent you from leaving. I am curious however, why you would choose to combine steroids with alcohol given your health condition because prolonged use of steroids and alcohol use can cause digestive issues, peptic ulcers, cirrhosis, or liver failure. For an individual who required a liver transplant, one would think you might take care not to consume alcohol at all... much less drink enough to be considered incapable of operating a vehicle.

The link below is to an article regarding the possible ramifications of combining steroids and alcohol:

https://americanaddictioncenters.org/alcoholism-treatment/steroids/

Per the Greeneville Sun's article about this incident, it stated that you feared for the safety of your dogs... that you were afraid   JOHN   and/or the unnamed male that was also present might harm your pets. Interestingly enough, I recall reading that BENJAMIN was arrested last year for animal cruelty and abuse. Authorities found dead cats and dogs on his property and inside of the home. Perhaps you had good reason to fear for the safety of your animals?

2. BENJAMIN & FL

According to several Facebook posts, comments and replies, and photos...
BENJAMIN did make his way down to FL. Ironically, records indicate he was even employed by a dog grooming

company in FL. Guess that company didn't do a very thorough background check, eh?

3. Vonda Smith's Assault

You stated in your point #6 reply regarding the rumor that JOHN allegedly assaulted Vonda Smith that, "There was no evidence..." and "[JOHN] was not even in town." You also stated that the TBI verified "all [of it]". Now, my team and I are intensely curious about these statements because #1: The incident did not occur in town, #2: How in the world did you conclude there was no evidence? And

#3: The TBI didn't verify shit because the incident was never investigated because it was never reported.

Prior to me initially writing about this alleged assault on Reddit, only four other individuals knew any of the details... including the alleged identity of Vonda Smith's attacker, `JOHN` .

So tell me... are your statements about this fabricated or have you unknowingly been fed false information by someone who might have been present during the attack?

4. Gary Ealey & The Morrison's

You stated that, "[Jessie's] family loves JOHN" but that hasn't always been the case, has it? Isn't it true that Jessie and JOHN ended up living at Cross Anchor because Jessie's mother, SUSAN, disliked JOHN and did not want him around or in her home? It has been witnessed that JOHN and SUSAN did not have a good relationship prior to Jessie's death.

I would like to say that my team and I only want the truth about what happened with this case and the current path you and I are on with these conversations might lead us down the wrong rabbit hole. If you can believe that Vonda Smith did not commit this crime, we can put our theory that JOHN committed this crime to rest. Maybe if we work together, we can come up with a theory actually worth pursuing. Let me know. Feel free to message me privately.

9 notes

I ultimately sent Christy a private message on Tumblr…

thealiensknow

Listen… I'm not the asshole I appear to be with this blog. I decided to spearhead this thing because Vonda's family was freaking out after her conviction (and rightly so) and they didn't have a clue what to do. So I jumped in to try and help. I don't want to be the person that airs everybody's dirty laundry like this or who points the finger in every direction and I certainly don't have any experience with any of this... I've just been taking every avenue to try and figure out what really happened

thealiensknow
I have really put myself in danger by writing this blog, but it had to be written. I had no idea that it would have ever of gotten the attention

it has. I joined Reddit as an outlet to map out the process my team and I were going through. No, it hasn't been "fair" to snoop on everybody and their mother... literally... but everything we found was public already. In this kind of situation, it's hard to differentiate between the good guys and bad guys. All of our research and reading and snooping and leads took us down, what we like to call, rabbit holes.

Dozens of rabbit holes. We started with several people (suspects) and would check them off basically, if we felt they weren't ultimately involved. A lot of people we looked into do have criminal records and shady pasts and that was a problem for us because it did make them suspicious to us. If I could go back, I would never have gotten involved, but I did. There is an innocent woman facing life in prison and there's a young pregnant mother without justice... so we keep trying. It's not pretty... I know that it's not... but I'm just a normal chick... trying to figure out what happened. And honestly, it was entirely about clearing Vonda in the beginning, but I was learning about Jessie and what happened to her and it started weighing very heavy in my heart... to the point of having nightmares about her dying. I didn't even know her.

If you know anything about any body or even just a gut feeling about any of it... please help us. Currently my team has been working on a new theory. It involves a house on Jud Neal Loop. Do you have any reason to believe Jessie would have been at a house on that road that day?

@CHRISTY
I'm not really sure when you sent this message but I just

now seen it. I understand what you are saying and it's a good thing to want to know the truth. Truthfully I don't like getting involved in any of this simply because I did not know either woman, I only said something because my husband doesn't deserve to be talked about as if he is scum of the earth. He may not have been the nicest person at times, in any of his relationships, but who has? I've known him for ten years so I feel I can say with confidence he doesn't have the heart to hurt someone, especially a child he believed was his. As far as Vonda, I have no feelings. I simply believe if she is guilty she should accept her punishment with Grace. If she is innocent, she should keep fighting as should those who are advocating her innocence. And to your question about a home on just Neal loop, the only thing

I ever heard was there was a woman who lived close to where she was found, that someone believed she may have been involved. No real evidence, just hear-say.

thealiensknow
I did not know Jessie or Vonda personally either. I would never blindly defend anyone against anything.
I made sure I did my homework before concluding (in my opinion) that Vonda

is innocent. Going through possible suspects is going to make me a bad guy no matter how you slice it... It hasn't been pleasant to do. My team and I no longer have reason to believe JOHN had anything to do with Jessie's murder. We still feel Vonda didn't either. We want to help Vonda AND Jessie... no matter the path it leads us down. If there's a woman that lives on Jud Neal Loop or frequented that area... we need the help. We have a great group of people involved with solving this case now, but we always welcome any info anonymously or otherwise. The blog on Tumblr is just the blog... the investigation is private and so are any tips.

 **@CHRISTY**

Wish I could help but I don't have a name I just remember somebody mentioning a woman in that area who's name was mentioned and that person had some reason to believe the woman was involved

thealiensknow
Well if you think of the name of the woman or anything else that comes to mind, you know how to reach me. Congratulations on your baby by the way ;)

I just want to point out that the "team" I refer to in my blog posts mostly refers to me and my mom, but at the start of our work on this case Vonda's family members were helping us as well. Jimmy has been a great help, too, and let's not forget the producers. My relationship with the producers, however, is mostly a one-way street, meaning I give them information and they take it. They did launch their own investigation into this, so it would be inappropriate for them to keep me in the loop about their work. Regardless, I intentionally used the term "team" throughout my blog because I needed people to assume I had at least a few people working on this with me.

    My aim in banking on peoples' assumptions about the number of people a team might consist of was for my protection, not my ego. I reasoned that if certain readers believed I had a group of people helping me, my chances of encountering danger might be limited. So I haven't necessarily lied. I do have a team, but I allowed peoples' imaginations to make assumptions. This little "gimmick" worked particularly well on my rival blogger, Hailey. Not that she believes I have a team, but her rage about it is comically priceless. The following exchange of ours highlights this:

HAILEY January 10, 2019 at 6:45 PM

I don't have time to play Freddy FUCK around with you. Yes I used a curse word. I don't have to be professional in a personal blog. Your "team" is ridiculous. If you don't like me calling out the nonsense you post that upsets Jessie's family then stop writing it. Stick to facts. If you write facts I will be more than happy to never mention your "team" (I can't even type that without laughing)

HAILEY January 10, 2019 at 6:49 PM

Now I'm finished playing around with you. Goodnight

My reply to Hailey...

Anonymous January 10, 2019 at 7:03 PM

Geezus Murphy you sure anger easily. What should I call the people that have been helping me if not "team"? Group? Posse? Gang? Buddies? If you and everyone else will chill out... on my blog, beneath the title, it specifically states that my blog is "An anecdotal story about a murder case". Do you have a dictionary? Would you like me to define "anecdotal" and "story" for you? Why are you such an angry person? You should really try meditating... or yoga. I've heard lavender essential oil is good as well as Lemon Balm supplements. I don't think we will be conversing beyond this last post.

Here we have a lady who also jumped in to make a comment and try to insult me, but my reply below her comment either went over her head or shut her up because she never did comment again.

Beth F January 10, 2019 at 7:33 PM

OMG, I never noticed that subtitle before! Wow..it all makes so much more sense now! Skim reading got me again, thanks for pointing it out here tonight. Puts a new perspective on the whole thing! See, I knew clearing the air would be a good thing.

Anonymous January 10, 2019 at 8:01 PM

Yes... it is always good to clear the air. Now we can plainly see the division between the idiots who require a disclaimer disguised as a subtitle and the intellectuals who do not.

What Hailey and many of her followers never could comprehend with their teeny tiny brains is that I'm not a professional. I stated over and over again that I am not a professional in any regard (which was thrown in my face a few times) and that I was only trying to figure out what truly happened to Jessie so that I could help free Vonda.

I'm sure I've made myself look like a bad guy, pointing the finger and whatnot, but listen up folks, if I'm pointing the finger at some piece of shit who has a criminal record and who's involved with drugs and/or violent crimes, then yeah… I'm gonna point my finger all day long at those types of people. As far as I'm concerned, they're a waste of breath as it is because I have absolutely zero empathy for fuck-ups.

Additionally, if you don't want me talking shit about you, then stop being shit. If you have a criminal record and your Facebook is public, then that shit is on YOU.… I simply took advantage of your ignorance. You bred yourself as fair game.

Chapter Six

What I consider fair game and what actual professionals consider fair game is relatively the same. I found this out the hard way. It was early in 2019 and I had been sending the producers e-mail after e-mail loaded with all kinds of information over the last several months. I had the privilege of dining with Caitlyn, Abby, and the Nashville investigator, Maggie, sometime in February 2019 and they eventually came back to town sometime later that March. This time, they brought "Ian."

I had never heard of the Wrong Man series before because we don't have cable, but sometime after the producers notified me that the Starz network had approved Vonda's case to be featured on the series, I decided to download the Starz app and watch Wrong Man for myself. After watching all the available episodes, there was one guy who stood out to me... Ian. He was so cool with his fedora and suave in the way he conducted himself.

As it turns out, Ian was once a police officer in Detroit until he, himself was wrongfully convicted of murder. He spent some time behind bars and when his name was eventually cleared he vowed to help others who were wrongly convicted. Ian is an investigator and interrogator. As an interrogator, he reads between the lines of what people are saying and he also reads their body language.

I would imagine an interrogator uses a variety of tactics to uncover the truth and, being a girl who loves military, spy and crime dramas, I suspect a large percentage of interrogating involves psychology. I studied psychology in high school and understand the basics. Being a Virgo (if you're into astrology), I have a naturally inquisitive and analytical mind. I also happen to be incredibly philosophical. These character traits of mine have helped me with this case and also proved handy once Ian came to town.

Vonda's eldest son Wyatt is Manning's father. I had met him once at a get together in Limestone when I first moved to Tennessee from South Carolina. There were maybe seven of us at a friend's house, drinking and listening to music. The mood was low-key, nothing rowdy or crazy, but this guy was passed the hell out pretty early on. I remember his girlfriend at the time, Jemma's mom—we'll call her Janet—was ready to go home, but their vehicle was stick shift and she couldn't drive it. With Wyatt passed out, this girl was stuck there until a friend came and picked her up. That was my first impression of Wyatt and it wasn't a good one.

Fast forward to the start of our gumshoe investigation after Vonda's conviction, and you can bet your ass Wyatt was on our list. My mom and I were suspicious of him, despite him being cleared as a suspect by the Greene County Sheriff's Department. Wyatt didn't have a Facebook profile for us to snoop on, and even though his girlfriend (who was likely no longer his girlfriend by the time Vonda was convicted) was helping us and providing us with tons of valuable information, I never did ask her about him. I might be ruthless at times when it comes to the truth, but I felt that asking her about Wyatt would just be too close to home for her. I was just getting to know her and didn't want to scare her away or piss her off, so Wyatt was never really mentioned at that time.

What did we know about Wyatt? I heard he might have been involved with a certain hobby and that he could be a heavy drinker, and I had witnessed that for myself at that get together in Limestone. We knew he had been in a relationship with Jessie at one point and eventually had a child with her. I learned that he was never really a part of Manning's life and that Jessie didn't necessarily want him to be. Apparently, Wyatt never told his family that he had a child with Jessie. Vonda found out about Manning through the grapevine, and once she did, she created a Facebook account so that she could find Jessie's profile and see a photo of her grandson. I'm not sure how or when Vonda contacted Jessie, but by the time she did, Manning was already a year old.

This was the start of Vonda and Jessie's relationship. Wyatt, on the other hand, had no relationship with Jessie and, to my knowledge, only saw his son every now and again. Wyatt's girlfriend at the time, Janet, became close friends with Jessie, as did Wyatt's brother and sister-in-law. Manning was surrounded by family and incredibly loved, as was his younger brother, Sam, when he came into the world approximately a year or so after Manning was born.

After Jessie's death, Wyatt's whereabouts were questioned, but law enforcement soon realized he had an alibi. He was with his then girlfriend Janet at a house party in Limestone, the same house where I had first encountered Wyatt years before. Additionally, his DNA wasn't found on Jessie or at the crime scene and he didn't appear to have a motive to murder her. There was a lot of talk around town about how Wyatt was probably involved somehow and many people speculated that Vonda was covering for him. Based on what we knew about him and the facts of the circumstances, my mom and I didn't pursue Wyatt as a lead because we really had nothing to go on and no clear reason to do so.

By the late summer of 2018, I had met with several of Vonda's family members to get information from them and notes for our work on the case and for my blog. Wyatt was the elusive missing link and I definitely wanted to meet him. Not only did I have questions for him that needed answering, I knew that an "interview" with him would be sensational for my blog because of the mystery and rumors surrounding him. As luck would have it, he ended up falling into my lap. One day, out of the blue, I found out that Wyatt had moved into Vonda's sister-in-law's house. I was stunned to learn that Wyatt was just down the road from me! I couldn't believe it! I was even more stunned when, one summer evening, Pam, Dale and their daughter came for a visit and Wyatt emerged from the car with them.

I was out front with my kids when they pulled up and my dog was outside with us, too. Looking at her, she looks like the cutest and friendliest dog (and she really is), but if you're a stranger, especially a male stranger, she will certainly go after you. My dog turns very scary very quickly at the sight of a stranger and she doesn't hesitate to run after you, growling and barking viciously. She's nipped ankles and has bitten a few, too. I'm ashamed to say that I have zero control over her when she's in protection mode. When I saw Wyatt (a male stranger) get out of the car, my immediate instinct was to grab my dog before she saw him.

To my absolute astonishment, my dog didn't go running or barking after Wyatt. She never even made her notorious low growl at him. I was blown away by her calm and accepting behavior. When I saw her reaction, I was intrigued. We all made our way out back to situate our chairs and our coolers so we could sit and chat. Immediately, I sensed Wyatt had good energy, on top of my dog evidently realizing it, too. I can't really explain it, but even in the first few minutes of being in his company, it felt as though we were instantly connected somehow. Was this the same guy I had met years ago at the house in Limestone? Was this the guy the town was judging and fussing about?

My observation of him that evening was that he was social, happy, funny and attentive. He got everybody's chairs out of the car and set them out back for them and then he went back and retrieved the cooler. He was even extraordinarily friendly with my kids and especially with my little guy, who had recently turned two and was quite shy around strangers. Amazingly enough, even my shy guy wasn't being bashful and seemed to take to Wyatt right off the bat. It was immediately evident to me that Wyatt was good people and certainly not a murderer. Later, when he met my cat, my freaking cat loved him, too! This was the start of our friendship.

Initially, when Wyatt first came over that summer evening, I decided not to mention the case or ask him any questions related to it. My intuition told me to befriend him before getting into all the shit, and that's exactly what I did. As the weeks passed by, Wyatt would often accompany Pam and Dale over to our house on the weekends to hang out and drink beer. We would typically have a bonfire when the sun went down, and we'd listen to music and drink and have a good time.

Eventually, the case did come up and when it did I was careful about easing my way into questions about it with Wyatt. I told him about my work on the case and that my mom was helping me, and I told him about my blog. Surprisingly, Wyatt was really open about what he knew, who he knew, and who he used to be. I had gained his trust enough for him to tell me a whole slew of shit and never once did I ever feel I had a reason not to trust him or what he told me. Wyatt was no longer a potential suspect or prized addition to my blog, he was my friend… the only friend I really had in Tennessee. My son was smitten with him and took to calling him "Uncle," which completely warmed Wyatt's heart. They became two peas in a pod, and I could tell that Wyatt really cherished spending time with my little guy because it filled the part of his heart that should have been filled by his own son, Manning.

Three days after Jessie's death, her mother, Susan, filed for emergency custody of Manning (and possibly Sam). Upon being notified about her filing, Vonda accompanied Wyatt to court the very next day, where he filed for full custody in response to Susan's actions. Just a couple of days later, Susan was awarded emergency custody of presumably both Manning and Sam and was accompanied by an officer over to Vonda's to retrieve them. Rumor has it that Susan allegedly smelled like a brewery when she came to get her grandsons. That was the last time Vonda ever saw the boys. Over the course of the next several months, Wyatt worked with an attorney in an attempt to get custody of Manning, but to no avail.

It appeared on Facebook as though Susan might have custody of both boys, despite Sam's father Shane having moved back from Texas and being available to be a father to his son. He also has young daughter with another woman in Texas and, based on some of his Facebook posts, that baby-mama allegedly won't let Shane have anything to do with their daughter. Shane might not have contact with his daughter in Texas, but that doesn't explain why he's not in his son's life here in Tennessee. He kind of makes it seem like his daughter is more important. An example of this can be found in a Facebook post he made just a day or two after Susan had been arrested for driving while intoxicated with Sam in the vehicle. Shane didn't post about his son, he posted about how much he missed his daughter.

While we're on the topic, let's talk about Susan's little run-in with the law before we get back to the ranch. It was the night before Christmas and all through the house... just kidding! It was the night before Easter of 2019. Ya know what? I think my Tumblr posts say it best, so here they are:

Posts	Likes	Following

Post #73

1/1 **SUSAN**

Well well.... if this isn't a conversation starter, I don't know what is. What were young children doing out after midnight and in a vehicle driven by a drunk? On the eve of Easter morning... children should be fast asleep and cozied in their beds while the parent(s)/guardian(s) busily set out colorful Easter baskets and hide little nests of plastic Easter grass and dyed eggs and candy. Instead of these children waking up to a morning full of love and childhood magic... they woke up to Grandma going to jail. Is this how SUSAN honors her daughter's memory? Is this the value she has for human life?

What will happen to the children?

Post #74

"I Can't Even..."

Crack a cold beer, sleuths... we got to talk.

(*crack a cold beer if you're NOT driving)

I can't seem to let this recent news slide off my back. Can't shake it... for a lot of reasons I suppose.

Why did SUSAN have a 3 and a 6 year old out so late?

Why would she choose to drink and drive with children in the car?

Why would she have them out so late and drunk driving the night before Easter morning?

Why would SUSAN, after losing her daughter, make the choice to risk the lives of others, of children, when she knows that pain all too well?

I think this scenario bothers me for the above mentioned questions and more.

Here we have a legal problem...
a substance problem... a safety problem... a moral problem... and a

spiritual problem.

SUSAN broke the law. It is against the law to drink and drive. An individual who can not remember when they started drinking or how much they drank has a substance problem. A drunk who just got busted for driving under the influence of alcohol with young children in the car has a substance problem. A drunk who smiles in her mugshot photo in spite of these circumstances... has a substance problem. The circumstances of drunkenness pose a safety problem for the children in her care and custody. And considering she was driving on the open road... strangers' lives were also at stake. Morally speaking, this was a huge lack of judgement on SUSAN's part. What exactly are her morals? Her mugshot smirk suggests she has none.

We live in a day and age where things are changing rapidly. Where ego has replaced consideration... self-centeredness has replaced selflessness and where self preservation replaces humanity. We live in a time when #mytruth replaces THE truth. These are all spiritual problems. We are (collectively) so far away from, so out of sync with the divine, that we forget what it's all about... what life is and what it's value is.

We gotta do better... we gotta be better... and we're only as strong as our weakest link. And to me, every human is a link in the chain, so when there's injustice... it bothers me.

SUSAN's choice to drink and drive was a bad choice. SUSAN's choice to drink and drive LATE the night before Easter with two young children in the vehicle and being a mother who has already lost her own daughter and is the legal guardian of her daughter's son (possibly SONS)....... is an epic no-no.

Now let's get back to the ranch where boy meets world. As summer faded into fall and fall faded into winter, Wyatt continued to come over on the weekends and hang out with me and my husband. He told me all kinds of stories and those stories are only allegedly true, so let's all keep that in mind as we go through them. My intention is never to destroy a person's reputation. I'm simply painting a picture to help illustrate what their character might be like.

More to the point, and this is my official disclaimer: the individuals I talk about in this book have presumably already ruined their own reputations because of their own actions. If you don't want people talking shit about you, then don't be a criminal and don't have a public Facebook profile, it's that simple. Public information is public information. Additionally, and this is the big one, kids, every individual is innocent until proven guilty. That means that no matter what their arrest record looks like or whether they've even been indicted (formally charged for a serious crime), they are still innocent of said crime(s) until proven guilty in a court of law.

Now, here's your story, sleuths: Once upon a time, a boy met a lady called Mrs. M. The pair were introduced by Mr. Dope, who they were mutual friends with. One day, Mrs. M introduced the boy to her daughter and the boy and girl began dating. Their relationship didn't last long at all, but little did they know, there was something baking in girl's oven. At some point, Mrs. M decided the boy had to go. He had allegedly been living in Mrs. M's house and they allegedly fought over their friend, Mr. Dope. He was always the life of the party and he was so popular that people allegedly paid either Mrs. M or the boy to hang out with him.

Evidently, more people had allegedly been paying the boy to hang out with Mr. Dope than they were paying Mrs. M and this allegedly hurt Mrs. M's feelings, which is why she allegedly kicked the boy out of her house.

Years later, the boy made a new friend called The Writer, to whom he told a story about Mrs. M. The Writer listened intently as the boy explained that Mrs. M allegedly had special friends called Sirens. The Sirens would allegedly visit Mrs. M to hang out with Mr. Dope. Sometimes the Sirens would allegedly bring their friends Jackson, Grant and Franklin to party with Mr. Dope and Mrs. M. On other occasions, the Sirens wouldn't invite Jackson, Grant or Franklin to hang out at all; instead they brought their friends the Womb Brooms to the party at Mrs. M's. The Womb Brooms were really popular, too, and so sometimes they would trade places with Mr. Dope. And, in doing so, everyone could enjoy themselves and have a good time with good friends.

The boy went on to tell The Writer that Mrs. M even allegedly had a good friend called Gavel. Gavel was a good 'ol boy who had known Mrs. M and her friends the Sirens for a long time. He was such a kind friend to Mrs. M that when she found herself in trouble, he allegedly came to her rescue. Gavel was especially special because he allegedly had two important groups of friends. One group was called The Suits and the other group was called The Bowties. The Writer considered the boy's story and allegedly wrote it all down. The end.

Now, may I present to you the mindbender, Ian. Sometime in March-ish of 2019, Ian came to town with the producers, and while here he wanted to meet Wyatt. The plan was for Wyatt to meet him at a hotel in town. OK, not sketchy at all. Wyatt had major reservations about meeting with Ian, but I told him not to worry so much because Ian was coming here to help. The day came and Wyatt ultimately went to meet Ian. After each man introduced himself to the other, Ian allegedly asked Wyatt to remove his boots and shake them out. Wyatt allegedly got patted down and was then allegedly instructed to shake each leg, presumably to cause anything to fall from his pant leg in the event he might have had a weapon or a wire or whatever the hell.

Next, Ian offered Wyatt a seat at a table, where he took a seat across from him. Wyatt was nervous to be talking to someone of such caliber but was mostly nervous because his intuition had told him not to go and I'd convinced him to anyway. What happens when you get nervous? Your palms fucking sweat like a whore in church. Wyatt rubbed his palms on his jeans in an effort to dry them. Immediately following the drying of the palms, Wyatt slid his hands into his pant pockets because he got cold.

He later told me that the hotel room was freezing because the air conditioning was blasting and, in complete fairness, Wyatt's skinny ass does not do well in any temperature below, like, 78 degrees. He hates the cold. He always seems to be cold and he does a good job bitching about being cold, so I was not surprised in the least that he plummeted his bare hands into his pockets to try to stay warm. Ian, however, must have allegedly gotten spooked by Wyatt's movements because as soon as Wyatt's hands went into his pockets, Ian allegedly told him to take them back out.

Once Wyatt's hands were visible again, Ian allegedly instructed Wyatt to empty his pockets onto the table, which he did. To be fair, Ian allegedly emptied his pockets as well. Finally, the interrogation, erm… conversation could get underway. Ian allegedly asked Wyatt a crap ton of questions, allegedly gave him a lie detector test and allegedly quoted to Wyatt statements from sealed, private medical records. I'm no attorney and neither is Wyatt, but we were very curious as to how Ian came to possess such records. Nevertheless, he allegedly had them and there was nothing for Wyatt to do other than to tell the truth, the whole truth and nothing but the truth, so help him God.

Ian allegedly became very confused as to Wyatt's whereabouts the day of Jessie's murder. Wyatt explained to him that he and his then girlfriend Janet lived together and shared a single car between them. His girlfriend had taken the car to work that day, leaving Wyatt home alone until approximately 6:30pm when she returned home from work. Wyatt has told me that he doesn't remember ever leaving the house that day, and that he also doesn't remember what he did. From an interrogator's standpoint, I'm sure that when an individual "can't remember," it throws up a red flag. But here's the deal with that… through no fault of their own, many of Vonda's relatives and family members can't remember shit. I know this because I've battled with that exact problem for over a year now. In order for me to work on this case, I must sometimes rely on their memories of things. I have continually been faced with enough of the "I can't remember," "I'm not sure" and "I forget" replies to last me a lifetime, and I have frequently become enraged and have broken down in tears over my frustration with their incapacity to remember accurately, if at all. So, Ian, I feel your pain, my friend.

The difference between Ian's perspective and my own about this particular situation is that I know these people. I've become accustomed to their nuances and he hasn't. So what became another eye-roll for me became a red flag for Ian. He saw the red flag and ran with it right down a rabbit hole. This seemed to launch a whole new problem for me, and it only got worse as the weeks wore on.

Chapter Seven

Vonda's conviction in May 2018 obviously warranted an appeal. Her attorney, Steven, filed for one following the trial and the hearing for her appeal had been scheduled for August 4th, 2018. Due to the trial transcripts not being ready yet, Vonda's hearing for an appeal was pushed to sometime in January 2019. Days before her hearing, it was cancelled because there was a typo in the trial transcript and because someone hadn't filed the necessary paperwork for her transport. Finally, her hearing for an appeal was set for May 2nd, 2019 at 9am. Then it was rescheduled for the following day at 11am.

I did not attend the hearing due to safety reasons (I didn't want to risk my identity), but my family reported back as soon as the hearing concluded. The appeal was denied. The producers were there and were, amazingly enough, allowed to film inside the courtroom. Both before and after the hearing, the producers spoke (on camera) to Vonda's family and supporters and Jessie's family and supporters. I was told Hailey was there as well (of-freaking-course she was).

I was told Vonda limped her way into the courtroom and was nearly unrecognizable. Evidently, she had lost a lot of weight and her hair had grown longer. To get an idea of how drastically Vonda had changed between her initial arrest and her hearing for an appeal, which only spanned two years, I've included side-by-side photos.

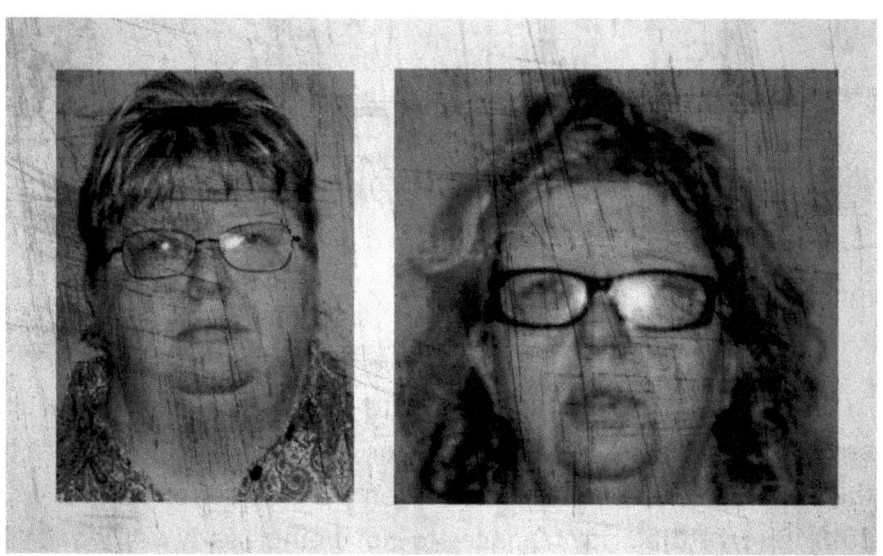

Hours after the hearing, I went over to Pam and Dale's house to visit. We talked some about the hearing of course, but Pam wasn't much in the mood to discuss it and Wyatt wasn't in the best place to even consider what had happened. But everything changed when I got an unexpected phone call. Pam and Dale's daughter called me with devastating news and it was up to me to break it to them.

Their daughter has a friend that works in the Greene County Detention Center and who had the chance to speak to Vonda after the hearing. What Vonda confided in that woman was heartbreaking. The woman told Pam and Dale's daughter what Vonda had told her, who was now on the phone telling me. She relayed to me that when Vonda, who is imprisoned in Memphis, was transported to Nashville by an employee of the prison in Memphis, she was then handed off to an employee of the Greene County Sheriff's Department, whose responsibility was to transport her from Nashville to Greeneville for her hearing.

Halfway to Greeneville, the man driving the police cruiser Vonda was being transported in somehow crashed into the back of another vehicle, presumably on the interstate. Upon impact, Vonda, who was asleep at the time, was hurled into the cage partition of the police cruiser. The driver and his colleague allegedly failed to buckle Vonda's safety belt at the onset of their trip. Vonda could not have buckled her own seatbelt due to her handcuffs and shackles. The police cruiser was allegedly totaled, and Vonda was then transported, by ambulance, to the nearest hospital. She was allegedly not given any pain medication, nor was she x-rayed or given an MRI. Vonda suffered a deep laceration of the scalp, just in the hairline, and was allegedly stitched up without any medication of any kind.

I took a deep breath and hung up the phone. I knew a Band-Aid is easier to remove if it's ripped off quickly, so that was my strategy. I returned to the porch where Wyatt and Pam and Dale were. I sat back down in my chair and waited a moment before ripping the Band-Aid off. Pam cried a bit and Wyatt just crumbled. I went over to him and hugged him and told him I was sorry. I called Abby, Caitlyn's assistant, afterward. I told her what we had learned about what happened to Vonda on her way to Greeneville and I gave her the name of the driver.

When I got home that night, I called my mom to give her the news. We immediately got on Facebook to snoop on the driver. Although his friends list was set to "private" so that it wasn't visible to the public, we did go through his posts and viewed the names of anyone who had commented on his posts or who had liked them. We were all too familiar with our growing list of names and we were curious to see if the driver was acquainted with anyone on our list. I think we did ultimately find a couple of people who raised our eyebrows, but the person that stood out the most was an individual who was a mutual friend of mine and the driver.

Janet was friends with the driver. I texted her right away to tell her what had happened to Vonda. When I told her who the driver was, she was surprised. I pointed out that she was friends with him on Facebook and because of that his friends list was visible to her. I asked her if she would scroll through it to see if he was friends with anyone of interest. To my surprise, she told me no. Her reason for not wanting to help was allegedly because the driver had over 300 friends on his friends list and she felt it would take too long to go through.

Wow. Um, OK. This chick doesn't have the time to surf through 300 faces, but here my mom and I are surfing through thousands and thousands of people, literally. It's not that I expect Vonda's family and friends to ask me how high to jump when I ask them for a favor, but in my mind, if they care about Vonda, they should be more than willing to help me help her.

This, unfortunately, has not always been the case. Many times I have asked for a favor or tried to delegate a small task just so my mom and I could have some help, but it never happened. And I was confused as to why. Not only was I confused, I was frustrated and angry. I'm working on this case to help YOU ALL, I would think to myself. It's their damn family member locked in prison for the rest of her life! My mom and I don't have a dog in this fight, but we entered the arena to help Vonda and her family. This took an emotional toll on me at times, but I trudged on with it in the name of justice. Going against the grain on this has proven difficult, unpopular and dangerous. Aside from earning the unpopular award for openly questioning this case in a small and potentially corrupt town, I might have become unpopular with Ian, too.

The producers and Ian had returned to Greeneville for Vonda's hearing for an appeal. And, during this trip, Ian got the opportunity to talk with Vonda face to face while she was staying in the Greene County Detention Center before being transported back to Memphis. The consensus was that Vonda was hiding something. From locals within the community to possibly the authorities to the producers and Ian, even to some family members, people generally believe that Vonda knows something that she's not telling. Sparking this notion was the fact that Vonda never took the stand in her own defense, even though legally that isn't supposed to mean anything. Still, to this day, nobody can really understand why. Vonda has made the statement that she's where she needs to be to protect her family. She has also made the statement that she plans to tell all, if and when she's granted a new trial. Based on her statements, we have no choice but to assume she does know something that she's not telling.

Vonda's "secret" propelled Ian's conversation with her that day in the county jail. He allegedly recorded their conversation and allegedly pressed Vonda to tell him who returned her car to her driveway the day of Jessie's murder. Vonda allegedly answered Ian's question. With his audio recording of their conversation in hand, Ian later played the recording for Vonda's husband, Don, and her sons, Wyatt and Curtis. He also played it for Vonda's sister-in-law, Pam, and her husband, Dale. From what I've been told, the recording is of Ian allegedly asking Vonda who returned her car that day and her allegedly replying that it was Wyatt. Seems like Vonda dropped a bomb, huh?

This is where my Virgo brain comes into play. Without having heard the recording myself, my knowledge and opinion is limited, and I'm left with questions, common sense and my imagination. My first question was, what exactly did the family hear in the recording? Was the audio of Ian asking who returned the car and then Vonda answering, "It was Wyatt"? Or was the audio of Ian asking who returned the car and Vonda saying, "Wyatt returned the car"? Yet again, I was met with silence and/or deer in headlight gazes. The family could not remember what exactly they had heard.

The difference in the phrasing of Vonda's reply is absolutely crucial. If Vonda can be heard in the audio replying, "It was Wyatt," then the recording could easily have been edited and altered. Vonda could have answered a different question entirely with her reply being, "It was Wyatt" and then, with a quick bit of editing, that answer could have been removed from the original question and replaced to appear as the reply to Ian's question about who returned her car. If, on the other hand, Vonda's reply was a complete sentence of, "It was Wyatt who returned the car," then Wyatt is presumably up shit creek without a paddle.

If Ian was here to help, why would he possibly edit and alter his own recording to make it seem as though Vonda was ratting out her own son? This technique, if it was truly applied, is a simple brain game and I'm betting that Ian was betting it would fool the family, even if just momentarily, so that he could see their reaction to it. A person's body language can sometimes speak louder and more truthfully than whatever is or is not coming out of their mouth. If the recording was allegedly edited with the intent to make it appear as though the jig was up for Wyatt, Ian would have walked away with the reactions of the family. And their reactions was exactly what he came to get.

It was crystal clear that Ian was after Wyatt. But was he unknowingly chasing a red herring down a rabbit hole? Just before Ian and the producers left town, Wyatt literally chased them down in his car because he had heard they'd stopped by Pam and Dale's house (likely to talk to Wyatt), but Wyatt was no longer living there. When Wyatt caught up to them, Ian's alleged parting words were, "You can run, but you can't hide." As haunting a statement as that is, I found it comical because it actually doesn't make any sense. I would say that a man who literally chases you down is not trying to run, or hide.

When this shit with the audio recording and the creepy statement to Wyatt happened, I decided it was high time that I contacted Ian. At this point, I had been working on the case for a year, I had been in contact with the producers for eight months, and yet, I had never been in contact with Ian. He was never included or copied onto a single e-mail I ever sent to the producers. I started to wonder if he was even getting all the information and leads I was sending the producers. Why was this guy so hung up on Wyatt? I had found a handful of violent criminals who could have had possible motives and who either knew Jessie or ran in shared circles and yet Ian was still seemingly after Wyatt.

I asked Pam for Ian's number and then haphazardly sent him a text message. I told him that we needed to talk. He replied, asking me who I was. I explained that I was the one who brought Vonda's case to Mr. Berlinger. Immediately he texted, saying he was available to talk. I called him. He was very nice and laid back on the phone, and although I tried to organize my thoughts to explain exactly why I was calling, I had a difficult time doing so. He was at a bar or restaurant and the background noise and chatter was incredibly distracting.

Ian asked me who I thought murdered Jessie and I told him that that was a difficult question, but that I had a list of names. He then asked me if I thought the suspect was male or female, to which I said I thought it was probably one or two males and one female. I told him that I really didn't think it was Wyatt and roughly explained why. Ian had told me that he was available to talk, but it was evident that he wasn't. He was in the middle of paying for his food and I could hear loads of chatter in the background. If I were him, I wouldn't have taken what could be an important phone call under those circumstances. He told me he was interested in talking with me some more and said he would call me the next day. The next day came and went, as did many more, and so far I haven't heard from him again.

I've learned that there really is no code of conduct in working on a murder case. I've also learned a cold reality… murder makes money. It is true that there's profit to be made from a tragedy, and if you're not making that profit, someone else will. This doesn't sound like me, does it? That's because it's not, but what I'm saying is true and I've learned that lesson tonight (July

19th, 2019). I recently announced on my Tumblr blog that I got a book deal about this case. I was waiting to tell Vonda's family about it until an appropriate time arose, but one family member found out before I could tell him myself.

I received a simple text message last night and it read, "Don't ever contact me again." It was from Wyatt. Then my husband got a text message from him that asked, "Are you home?" My husband called him immediately. Their conversation was brief. Wyatt was upset about my book deal because "they're out here struggling" and then hung up the phone. My husband, the nice guy that he is, wanted to assume the call simply dropped, so he texted Wyatt, to which there was no reply. I was confused, but nevertheless my suspicions had been confirmed.

In retrospect, I think I had been dragging my feet about telling the family I was writing a book about the case because a part of me sensed I would catch some flack for one reason or another.

The following day (today), I texted Wyatt and basically told him that writing a book about his mom's case was just another avenue to try to gain attention in hopes of it somehow helping her. I told him that I wanted people to know what was happening in Greene County and to have a little faith in me. You see, I thought Wyatt was referring to "the struggle" as in the emotional and mental struggle of coping with the mess of this case and that he was upset about this book being published because it might make matters worse. Hours later, I found out exactly why Wyatt was pissed and what "the struggle" really was, in his mind.

My husband called me pissed the hell off because he had apparently just had a texting war of sorts with Wyatt. Evidently, the struggle Wyatt was referring to was the alleged current financial struggle of his mom and dad. He feels that I owe them the money from any book sales. I replied with grace, despite his tantrum of seething greed. I told him that I wasn't even finished writing the book yet and asked him why he assumed I wouldn't help his mom and dad financially, if I could. I explained that him throwing this tantrum with his hand out for money would be like me throwing a tantrum with my hand out for any money Vonda might be awarded for being wrongly convicted. It simply isn't right and, quite frankly, it's trashy.

If anyone is left wondering if Wyatt's true colors have ended our friendship, the answer is yes. If anyone is wondering if I feel I owe anybody a single penny from the sales of this book (other than definitely owing my mom), the answer is no. I don't concern myself with money because I'm a simple person and I already have everything I need, but the reality of publishing a book is that there will eventually be money made and whether it's a little or a lot is beside the point because writers don't generally write for the money, we write because it's in our blood and we love it. More to the point, this isn't some tra-la-la fiction novel I'm writing for shits and giggles. A young, pregnant mother has lost her life and the life of her unborn baby. Jessie's two young sons have lost their mom. An innocent woman is serving life in prison. This shit is real and it's scary and it's happened to my family.

While we've drifted into a story inside of a story, we might as well linger here a bit before getting back to the book. Crack a cold beer, sleuths. The thing about writing this book right now is that shit is still unfolding out here in Greene County. I'm over here criss-cross applesauce on the ottoman I have pushed up against my kitchen window, drinking a beer and smoking a cigarette with my laptop's screen obnoxiously glowing at me, and I'm doing my best to get this story down. I'm finding that it's not so easy to write a story about something that's still unfolding, but we'll make it through, yeah?

So here's another little side story about something that just happened to me last week. I went to Wal-Mart, and just as I had pulled into a parking space, my toddler fell asleep. I decided to let him get a catnap before doing our shopping. I called my mom to chat with her for a bit while the little man slept. As we were chatting, I noticed a guy walking into the store that looked mighty fucking similar to JT. JT, to my knowledge, was supposed to be locked up. This guy had gotten taken down in a major, multi-agency drug bust back in October 2018 along with, like, 20 other people.

My mom and I continued chatting and soon enough out came JT's doppelganger and he's walking down the aisle in front of where I'm parked, so I could see him clearly. I said, "Mom, I think JT is at Wal-Mart! He's fucking walking right in front of me!" My mom, the freaking super sleuth and Johnny-on-the-spot, did a quick search that revealed that JT never showed up for court back in November following his October arrest. She said he had a warrant out for his arrest. Meanwhile, I'm surfing through his Facebook profile to compare JT's tattoos to the doppelganger in front of me and they're identical. Bravo, Greene County.

According to an online article regarding the multi-agency drug bust in East Tennessee back in October 2018, a federal grand jury indicted twenty-two individuals in a meth distribution conspiracy. Two of the players on our player list, JT and Chasity, were indicted. Remember, every individual is innocent until proven guilty. The article states that if they're convicted they each face a minimum mandatory sentence of at least ten years and up to life in prison. Chasity also faces a minimum mandatory sentence of at least five years and up to life in prison for firearms charges, if convicted.

So you tell me how JT is out free as a bird when he should be behind bars right now. An old friend of Pam and Dale's stopped by the other day. When he was told that I had seen JT at Wal-Mart, he wasn't surprised. The man said he knows JT and he told us that JT had allegedly rolled on some guys in a neighboring town. He alleged that JT is a snitch for Greene County and that might be why he's not locked up when he should be.

Let's run with this alleged rumor of JT being a snitch for Greene County. A snitch is a person who betrays others (usually other criminals) by ratting them out to authorities. A snitch is not a paid informant but might be rewarded with a favor or favors. On the other hand, a snitch can also be blackmailed for intel. Typically, people don't sign up to be a snitch, the job finds you in a manner of ways. I've heard rumors that allege Greene County has a few ways of creating snitches. An individual might be indoctrinated by means of a special ceremony, one I like to call extortion. Rumor has it that authorities around these parts sometimes allegedly stop vehicles of certain people (usually known criminals) and inform the driver of the vehicle that he or she is now going to work with the authorities on a particular matter, and if the driver seems unwilling, something like an unregistered handgun or a bag of meth can easily appear in the driver's possession.

There are, however, two ways to skin a cat. If you're not lucky enough to be christened a snitch in the comfort of your own vehicle by way of criminal evidence magically appearing in your possession, the opportunity to have this title bestowed upon you can allegedly find you in a place of false security. It is rumored that when drug addicts in this county go before a certain judge, whom we'll call Judge B, they are granted their freedom on one condition, he or she must attend a program at a very specific rehabilitation center (which I will not be naming). Dark tales have emerged about this place, with those that go there either remaining silent about their experience (presumably out of fear) or barely being capable of uttering a few words about it. I've read some Facebook profiles of our players and there have been two or three to make mention of such a place.

The rehabilitation center is allegedly more akin to "boot camp" or "training," as I've heard it referred to. This is where criminals get turned. When they're released from "rehab," some come out as snitches. Being a snitch is dangerous but can also offer some protection.

To the dangerous end, if and when others have caught on to you being a snitch they'll probably want to kill you. As far as protection goes, if you're a valuable snitch, then authorities are likely to try to keep you out of harm's way... whether that danger comes from other criminals or the law itself. As you might imagine, the relationship between the county and a snitch can be a complex one.

Crack a cold beer, sleuths! We're gonna dive into our third theory of what could have happened to Jessie. This particular theory will divide itself, sprouting a couple different theories within a theory, so hang on to your hats, my friends.

Jessie was approximately sixteen weeks pregnant at the time of her death. Counting back, the possible date range she had intercourse that resulted in her third pregnancy would have been between April 28th and May 13th 2016, depending on variables we do not have the details of such as the first day of her last menstrual period, when she ovulated, and how many hours or days conception took. According to an online conception calculator, and based on a 16 week pregnancy at the time of her death, the following offers suggested dates of intercourse and conception:

- The most probable dates of conception occurred between May 4th and May 8th

- The most probable dates of intercourse occurred between May 1st and May 8th

- Possible dates of conception could be between May 3rd and May 13th

- Possible dates of intercourse could be between April 28th and May 13th

The following is an inside look at what was happening in Jessie's life between March 2016 and early May. The text messages are between Jessie (her texts are on the left) and Vonda (whose texts are on the right). I've blacked-out Jessie's contact info because Vonda had her number saved as Jessie's sons' names rather than Jessie's and I've changed their names in this book for privacy. Please note the dates of each text message. The handwriting on the first text message is Vonda's.

John allegedly broke up with Jessie in early March, after allegedly taking some of her tax return money.

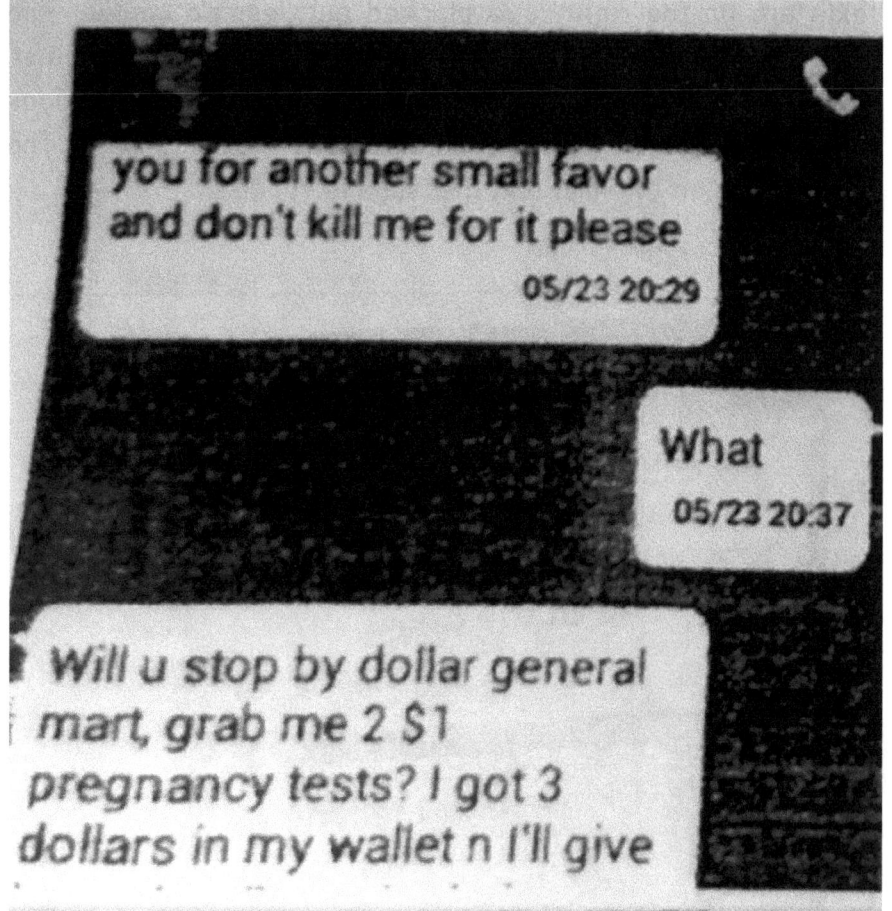

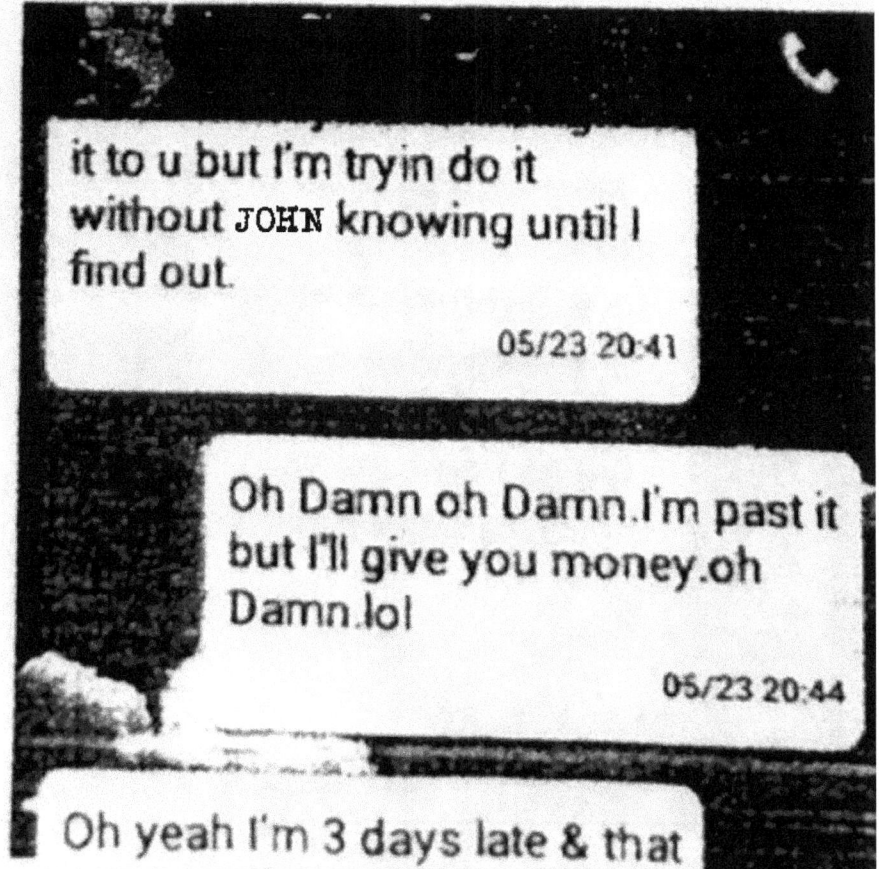

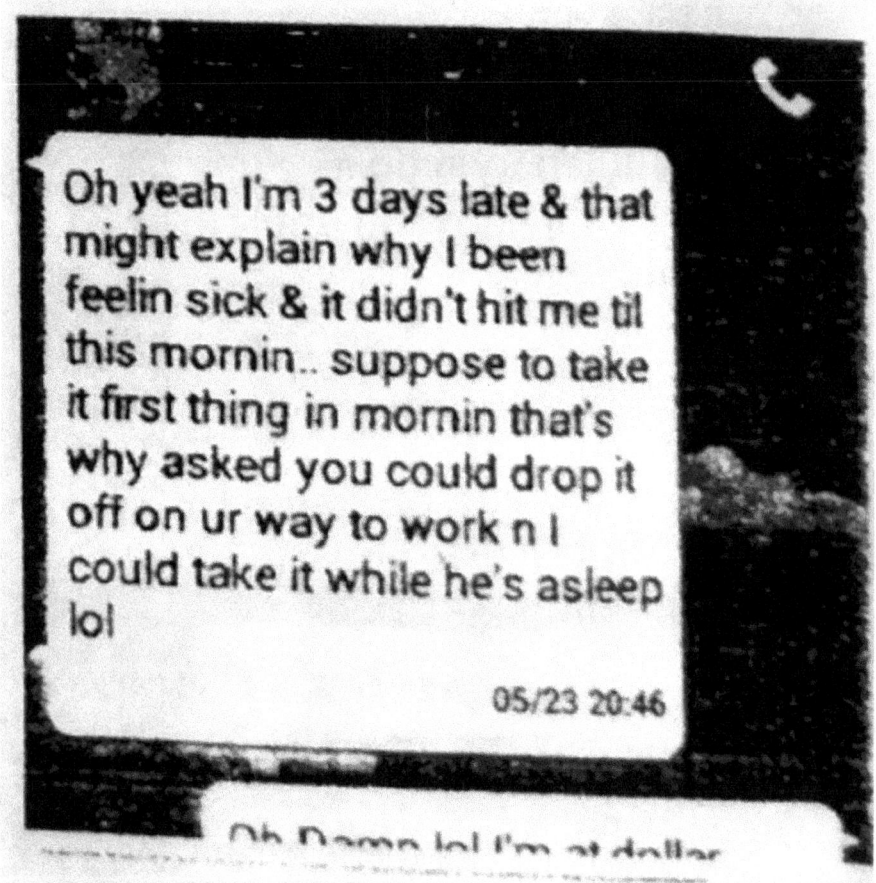

Ready for some math? On May 23rd, Jessie claimed that her menstrual period was three days late, which means she was expecting to get her period on May 20th. Most women's cycles average twenty-eight days between the first day of one period and the first day of the next period. So if her period was due May 20th, then the first day of her prior period started on approximately April 23rd and lasted 6-7 days. If her last period did in fact start on April 23rd, then she would have conceived between approximately April 30th and May 5th. If this is true, then Jessie was approximately 14—14 ½ weeks pregnant at the time of her death, which obstetricians would consider 16 weeks because all around the world pregnancy is gauged by the first day of a woman's last period rather than the actual date of conception because many times women don't know the exact date they conceived. That's another book though, not this one and not a book I'm ever going to write.

With a probable conception date between April 30th and May 5th, the question is… were John and Jessie back together by then or were they still broken up? If they were still broken up and Jessie slept with another man, then that might be why the DNA of the unborn baby has been kept a secret. Vonda's attorney Steven allegedly requested DNA testing be performed on the fetus to find out who the father was, but Judge Dugger allegedly denied the testing and therefore the fetus' DNA and the identity of the father was never mentioned during the trial. Why all the hush-hush surrounding the fetus? Most believe it's because that baby was not John's. Whose could it be? Could the answer to that be worth killing Jessie and her unborn baby? Welcome to our third theory, sleuths.

If Jessie slept with an unknown man and became pregnant with his baby, and that's why the fetus' DNA was either never tested or remains under lock and key, then we must ask ourselves who this guy could be and what makes his identity so worthy of protection. Many have wondered if the baby allegedly belonged to a cop or an individual with a reputation to lose. My crazy mom, who seems to have a penchant for Googling topics we joke will bring the feds knocking on her door because of her searches, discovered that pregnant women are more likely to be murdered than to die from complications of pregnancy. She also learned that when women commit murder, they typically do so because they have something to gain. Men, on the other hand, commit murder mostly due to emotional factors and ego, which is what is referred to as a crime of passion. The prosecution argued that Jessie's death was the result of a crime of passion, given her trauma and injuries. The top three reasons individuals commit murder are theft (financial greed), rape (sexual pursuit of power) and control. Murder of pregnant women is a type of homicide that usually results from domestic violence and is likely committed by a person the victim is close with, such as a relative, husband, boyfriend, lover, etc.

Jessie and her unborn baby's death encompass all three top reasons a person falls victim to homicide. Jessie had $1,000 cash on her, which checks the box for financial greed (and gain). DNA samples from her panties suggest she had been raped, which checks both boxes for sexual pursuit of power and control. Another check mark in the box for control could be her unborn baby's DNA and the identity of the father. Assuming the unborn baby belonged to someone other than John, that person could have murdered Jessie for one of two reasons. The first motive being the suspect didn't want the truth to come out about him being the father, and the second motive being the contrary; the suspect wanted to be in a relationship with Jessie and be a father to their baby, but Jessie ultimately went back to John.

Let's explore the second motive. Jessie's eldest son Manning was Wyatt's and, from the looks of the following text messages that Jessie sent to Vonda, Jessie didn't want Wyatt in Manning's life.

> **Jessie**
>
> I told you from the very beginning WYATT would never be around and you were fine with that and he knows that he fucked that up when he told me he didn't want nothing to do with him when he found out i was pregnant and ran like a lil bi*ch. he's not gonna try now to play daddy of the year.. he's worthless in my eyes.
> -j+q ♡

> **Jessie**
>
> support him cause your son was to damn sorry too. WYATT has no rights. nor will he ever. he made that decision when he found out i was pregnant at   on new years before I had him. and it's also his fuck up that he was to damn sorry to tell you and DON that he had a kid and that's why you guys missed all his life. i have nothing against you or DON i like you

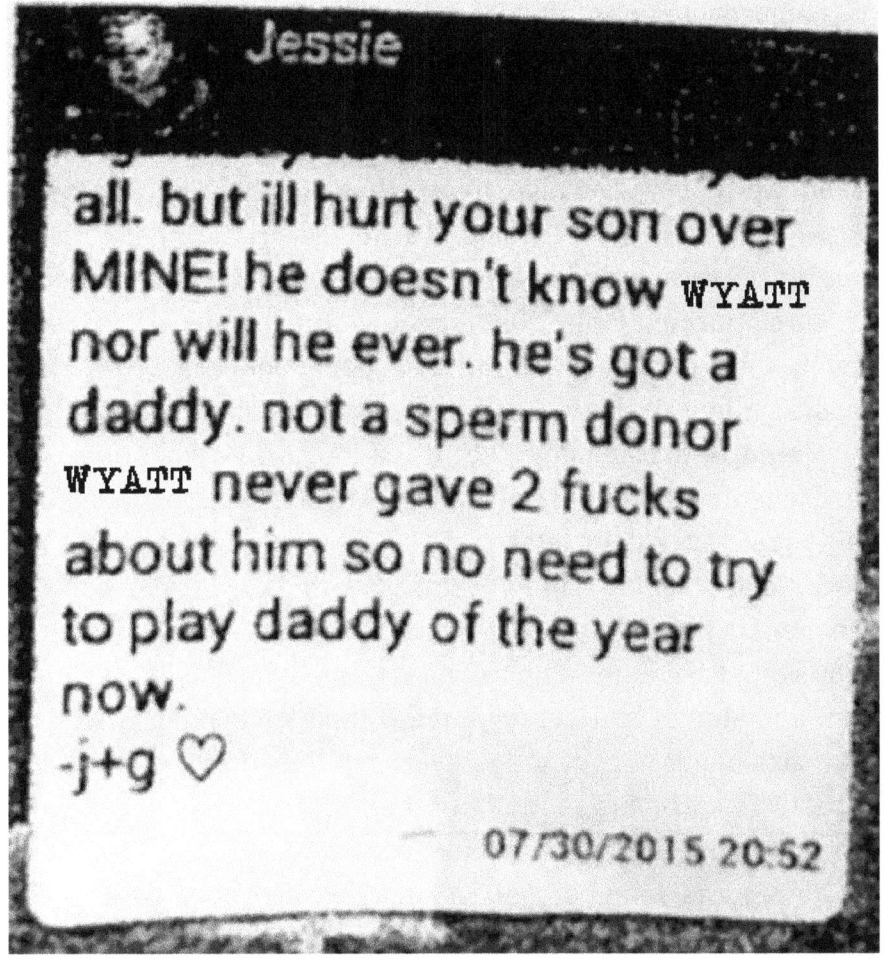

An important detail from one of these text messages is that Jessie states that she told Wyatt she was pregnant with his baby on New Year's Eve. Well, friends… Manning was born in February 2013. So Jessie was at a New Year's Eve party eight months pregnant and finally decided to tell Wyatt it's his child? When she's eight months pregnant?! Talk about dropping a bomb on somebody! Wyatt has told me in the past that Jessie allegedly uh… dated a lot. He claimed that Jessie wasn't even sure if the baby was his until after Manning was born and came out looking identical to Wyatt.

Fourteen months after Manning was born, Jessie became pregnant with Shane's son, Sam, who was born in December 2014. Manning and Sam are twenty-two months apart. Rumor has it that Jessie wouldn't let Shane or his family have anything to do with Sam. I've also heard that Jessie allegedly hated Shane's mother. If that's true, it's not surprising that Shane's mother (Sam's grandmother) was seemingly unaffected by Jessie's murder. I say that because the woman decided to update her profile photo on her Facebook the day before Jessie's funeral. Jessie and her unborn baby were brutally murdered, Sam tragically lost his mother to a violent crime, and his grandmother was preoccupied with posting a happy, smiling selfie just seven days later.

Sixteen months after Sam was born, Jessie became pregnant in May 2016 with her third child, rest its soul. The third baby would have been approximately two years younger than Sam and almost four years younger than Manning. It is evident that Jessie didn't really want Wyatt or Shane to be part of their sons' lives for one reason or another, so maybe she didn't want the father of her third baby to be part of its life either. After all, Jessie and John had gotten back together sometime in May 2016 after she conceived, and John was the father figure to both of her sons already, so maybe she decided she wanted things to remain that way. Before we explore the Mystery Man who might have gotten Jessie pregnant in May 2016 (if it wasn't in fact John), we need to understand the timeline of all the babies. According to Jessie's July 2015 Facebook relationship status, that's when she and John began dating. Maybe they were dating before then, but that's all we have to go on. If they did begin dating in July 2015, Manning would have been almost 2½ years old and Sam would have been just six months old. Interestingly, John and Britney's son was possibly born sometime in March 2016, which means he was conceived sometime in June 2015. So John knocks up Britney and the next month is in a relationship with Jessie. His and Britney's son is born in March 2016, and two months later he allegedly gets Jessie pregnant. Jessie and his alleged unborn baby are murdered just six months after his son with Britney is born. Let's have look at how Britney felt about all of this:

> **BRITNEY**
> He is almost 6 months now and i doubt any of you all are just going to walk in his life now. His sperm donor ain't even seen him but 5 times since he was born. He doesn't know any of you all:(JOHN is trash for him not to be a father. But raise everybody else's kids. Oh yeah that's right my children have my family thats it!

BRITNEY
I've never stopped JOHN from seeing him that's why he always went behind his jessie's back to sneak and see US even before i had him ive texts and pictures of him rubbing my belly. He has seen five times I've got it writin down the dates and how long he has spent with him. A total of five hours with 5 visits doesn't seam like he is trying very hard. Is the only one that had came to spend actual family time with him. Ans still does. Like today we have spent all day together if he would worry about his own children he would get farther IVE NEVER STOPPED

OR TOLD HIM THAT HE COULD NOT SEE HIS BLOOD CHILD! But he lets her controll him i cannot help who is raising his child he is a good father to both my boys and everybody sees it ask she actually comes around she has watched   grow knows his personality everything. And my mom said she has nothing from you and has not talked to you. Its JOHN'S decisions not mine ive done nothing but tried. Till i gave up. Its not going to be an argument though.

2013 — January: Jessie is 8 months pregnant and tells WYATT it's his
— February: Manning is born

2014

— March: Sam is conceived

— December: Sam is born

2015

— June: JOHN and BRITNEY conceive
— July: JOHN & Jessie begin dating

2016

— March: JOHN and BRITNEY's baby is born
— May: Jessie conceives third baby
— August: Jessie & 16 week old unborn baby are murdered

Now, my sleuths, let's get back to the ranch with this third theory and our mystery baby-daddy before we open the can of worms that is Britney.

We said that if Jessie's unborn baby truly belonged to a Mystery Man, this man could have had two opposing motives to want to kill Jessie. The first motive we're musing over is that Mystery Man wanted to be with Jessie and wanted to be a father to the unborn baby, but with this theory Jessie ditched him and went back to John and then found out she was pregnant. Jessie, as her track record somewhat indicates, either wasn't sure who the father of her third child was, or she was aware that the father of the baby was not John. Maybe the Mystery Man found out she was pregnant, did some math and assumed it was his. Maybe after failed attempts to win Jessie back, he finally snapped and killed her and the baby both. It could have easily been one of those "if I can't have you, no one will" scenarios. If Mystery Man killed them, how does he fit into the timeline and, more importantly, what about the white vans? There was an unknown male sample of DNA found in Jessie's panties and she did have three sets of unknown male DNA under her fingernails. Then there's the scenario where Jessie knows it's Mystery Man's baby and she confesses, both to him and to John. John could have become angry and killed her, but per the surveillance footage at his place of employment at the time, John was seen at work at 7:00pm that night.

Mystery Man's motive of wanting to be with Jessie and be a father and then being denied and killing them is a strong motive, but it's difficult to make him fit into the puzzle because of the white van Jessie was last seen getting into. Remember, both Bradley and Benjamin owned white vans at the time and I highly doubt Jessie had sexual relations with either of them.

Let's explore Mystery Man's possible alternative motive of killing Jessie and her unborn baby because he didn't want anyone to find out it was his. This particular motive for this theory also requires a stretch of the imagination, but let's go for it.

If you unintentionally got someone pregnant and were scared shitless of the truth coming out, what circumstances would warrant homicide to rid you of your problem? Let's examine the aftermath before we dive into Mystery Man's desperate need to hide his identity as the father. Judge Dugger denied DNA testing being done on the fetus to confirm or reveal the identity of the father. The unborn baby was never mentioned during trial. The prosecution claimed that Vonda's motive to kill Jessie was due to the fact that she had become obsessed with Manning and was upset that Jessie and John planned to marry, move away and start their own family. Yet, John's current wife, Christy, claims John and Jessie were never engaged. You see what I'm doing here? Judge Dugger refused to have the unborn baby's DNA tested, yet during the trial, the state was busy resting their motive on John and Jessie's happy little family life. Let's not forget about the day Vonda went snooping around in October 2016 to find out what really happened to Jessie and found herself beat up in a ditch the following morning. And how did Jessie's blood really find its way into Vonda's car? The point here is that this case is nothing shy of a massive cover-up, which might indicate that the county does know who the father of Jessie's unborn baby is and they're jumping through hoops to allegedly hide it.

If Mystery Man is important enough to have the county allegedly covering up the truth on his behalf, who the hell is he? What is he? Is this a situation where this Mystery Man is so fucking reputable that this would ruin him? Did he call on his friends to help make it go away, or is this a situation where Mystery Man's identity will open up a can of worms? A lot of times, if you pull one tiny thread of a lie, it begins to unravel in other places. If Mystery Man was found out, would that lead to other secrets becoming unearthed? In a small town and in a region where generations of families are woven together like a... whatever the hell is woven together, it's evident that all these good 'ol boys and good 'ol girls are in bed with one another, no matter their social status. Here, everything is a favor and often it seems that everyone's livelihood rests on favors. Doing a favor for someone out here means they owe you in the future, and people live and die by the favors they do and the favors they're owed. It's one hell of a barter system and it works out beautifully, unless you get screwed. The threads that weave these people together are family ties. The Southern term for this is "kin." People out here can be related in complex ways, as my mom and I have come to realize. It's like one big family tree in East Tennessee. Everyone seems to be kin to everyone, let alone everyone knowing everyone.

Family ties and favors come in especially handy for those in positions of authority, law, politics and business. So let's pretend Mystery Man falls in one of those categories. For the sake of giving him a title, we'll imagine Mystery Man is something lower on the totem pole of power. Let's say he's a cop. Now, how would Jessie cross paths with a cop, I wonder. Based on her post-partum toxicology report and what Wyatt has told me about her, Jessie did not use drugs. This fact narrows down how Jessie could have been introduced to an officer if she wasn't busy breaking the law. Her Facebook page revealed that she was friends with a cop just a bit older than her, but I doubt she would have been his type and he doesn't seem like the kind of man to get involved with someone who had kids.

When Jessie and John broke up in March 2016, they were living on Cross Anchor Park together. Presumably JT was also living there at that time. So who left the trailer after the breakup? I've asked around about this but haven't gotten a clear answer. We'll have to assume Jessie and her boys stayed on Cross Anchor. OK, so Jessie is going through an emotional breakup and she has her two boys to care for on her own now. Most people, when they go through a breakup, have their friends and family rally around them to help get them through it, right? They fill the void with time spent with those they love. So maybe Jessie and her boys found themselves spending more time at Vonda's house. Vonda has said, however, she generally stayed out of Jessie's business when it came to her romantic relationships, so it might be unlikely that Jessie found comfort in Vonda during this time.

Perhaps Jessie found herself spending more time at her mom's house. After all, when you're going through a breakup, sometimes you just want your mom. So, let's imagine Jessie and her boys were spending more time at Susan's house. What would that have been like? In order to paint a picture of life at Susan's, we'll need to explore her rumored lifestyle and the area in which she lives. Her lifestyle allegedly included friendships with officers and criminals, and her door was allegedly a revolving one. The middle-class neighborhood she lives in is mostly comprised of two-story homes with landscaped yards and appears like an average, all-American street, an ideal place to raise a family. My mom spent considerable time researching who the homeowners are on Susan's street and, on paper, it appears that many of Susan's neighbors could be considered influential. If Susan is friendly with her neighbors, she would have some connections worth bragging about. Even more so, if she's friends with some of her neighbors' friends.

Still playing pretend, let's imagine Jessie had been spending more time at her childhood home, and in doing so either was introduced to a special friend of her mom's or was reunited with one. This special friend is our Mystery Man and if he and Jessie began spending time together, they very well could have bumped uglies and unintentionally made a baby. Perhaps their union was a one-time deal and neither intended to enter a serious relationship. After all, Jessie did ultimately get back together with John in May 2016. The question is, did Jessie have a feeling she was pregnant and that's why she got back together with John, or was it just coincidental timing?

Fast forward a few months to August 12th, 2016, the day of Jessie's death. Perhaps Jessie was having doubts about the father of her then 16-week-old unborn baby, or possibly even guilt because she knew the truth. Maybe Jessie called the Mystery Man that day or a few days prior and told him she was pregnant, and she thought that it could be his. If this Mystery Man was a cop, as we imagine, he might have shit his pants at the news. Maybe this man had a family and maybe his position on the vast family tree would have caused major complications if it was learned he had fathered Jessie's baby. Mystery Man's fear of being connected to Susan's alleged lifestyle could have been one of those tiny threads of a lie I mentioned earlier, one that he couldn't afford to have pulled.

If mystery cop man truly did exist and truly found himself in a situation as I've described, he surely wouldn't want blood on his own hands. More likely than not, he would have made a panicked phone call, presumably to someone with more power than himself. This would have been one of those situations where kin and favors work together to protect one of their own. If you'll recall, those in power often have special relationships with the opposition around here. Criminals can come in handy and are easily blackmailed into doing others' bidding. Perhaps a phone call was made to JT or Bradley or someone else to take care of the situation.

If Jessie was pregnant with an officer's baby, it might explain why her cell phone was never found, despite it successfully being pinged and a location established. It might explain why the unborn baby's DNA has been kept secret and why it was seemingly so easy for John to move on after their death. It might also explain why Vonda was nearly beaten to death for her snooping and how Jessie's blood came to be in her car.

OK, back to March 2017. It was reported both on television and in the newspaper that Vonda Star Smith had turned herself in. This is, in fact, a slanderous lie. Officers had gone to Laughlin

Memorial Hospital hoping to find Vonda at work, but they did not see her car parked in the designated employee parking. The officers drove to her home on Davis Valley Road, but she was not home, either. There, they spoke to her husband, Don, who told them that Vonda was at work, but her car was parked elsewhere due to the employee parking lot being repaved. The officers had Don call the hospital to confirm she was there. Once Don got Vonda on the phone, he relayed the officers' message. She was to go down to the police station after work because they had a few questions to ask her. Vonda readily agreed and, rather than waiting until her shift was over, the law-abiding citizen and respectful person she is, she left work early and went down to the police station to answer their questions. Once there, Vonda wasn't asked any questions at all; she was arrested on the spot.

Chapter Eight

Vonda's car was searched, sealed and towed to TBI (Tennessee Bureau of Investigation) in the early morning hours following the night Jessie's body was found. Sheriff Pat Hankins contacted the district attorney regarding Jessie Morrison's murder case. He wanted to arrest Vonda Smith for the crime, but the D.A. allegedly warned him that he didn't have enough evidence to arrest her. Vonda was eventually arrested seven months after Jessie's death, in March 2017. According to a post-conviction statement made by state prosecutor David Baker who reflected on the start of the case, he admitted that there were many challenges in obtaining a conviction and ascertained that they wouldn't have succeeded if it weren't for the team that prosecutor Cecil Mills and Jeff Morgan organized. Sheriff Pat Hankins was credited with advocating for a first-degree murder indictment.

Let's talk about this plainly, shall we? Jessie and her unborn baby are murdered. Jessie's blood is allegedly found in Vonda's car, presumably either by the sheriff and detectives who initially searched her car or by TBI once the vehicle was in their possession. The sheriff allegedly tells the D.A. that he wants to arrest Vonda but is told there isn't enough evidence to make the arrest. In the first several months following Jessie's death, the state had shit to go on and yet magically that all changed when prosecutor Cecil Mills and Greene County Detective Jeff Morgan added Michelle Holt to the team in 2017. Shortly after this power team is organized, Vonda is arrested. Does this make sense to anyone?

If Jessie's blood was in Vonda's car on the same day Jessie was murdered and this is the only evidence that warranted Vonda's arrest and conviction, why then did the D.A. allegedly tell Sheriff Pat Hankins that there wasn't enough evidence to arrest her? Get my point? If the state had the evidence of the blood at the beginning of the case and still only had the same evidence of the blood at the end, then why was Vonda not arrested earlier? How did the state go from not having enough evidence (when they allegedly had the blood in the car) to that same lack of evidence suddenly being more than enough to arrest and convict Vonda? My personal belief, and it is a belief that many others share, is that the blood was planted.

Jessie's blood being planted in Vonda's car is the only rational explanation for the tide turning under circumstances that never changed. When did this "ah-ha" moment for the state occur? If blood was in the car from day one, and it was the blood in the car that sent Vonda to prison for life, what was the state's struggle with the case in the beginning? If you have a 200-piece puzzle but you only possess one puzzle piece at the start of assembling it, how on earth can that same single puzzle piece, months later, complete the entire 200-piece puzzle? To better understand this magic, we needn't look any further than the magicians. Detective Jeff Morgan, as luck would have it, just so happens to be John's uncle. State prosecutor Michelle Holt is married to a man named Wesley Holt, who was elected sheriff of Greene County in the summer of 2018, ousting Pat Hankins. Hankins himself one day allegedly had no evidence to arrest Vonda and then the next day, still armed with that same lack of evidence, arrested her.

Detective Randolph was the one who allegedly found items belonging to Jessie strewn along Betsy Ross Road and Tyne

Gray Road and was the one who investigated the location of the cell phone ping. Detective Randolph was also at the scene the night Vonda went missing in October 2016 and was the one who showed up at the hospital wanting to take Vonda's statement. Four magicians, each with their own bag of tricks.

Randolph might own a bag of tricks, but he also seems to possess supernatural powers. Vonda's sister-in-law, Pam, once told me a story about what can only be described as a display of psychic powers. Pam and her husband Dale had a nickname for Randolph, a nickname only the two of them had knowledge of and used for giggles between them. They referred to Randolph as Rudolph. Pam explained to me that she had gotten a call from a family member one day and that this family member, whom we'll call Terry, is long-time friends with Buddy Randolph. Terry told Pam that Randolph had stopped by to visit him. He went on to say that during their visit, Randolph told him that Pam and Dale call him (Terry) Rudolph. Confused, and having never heard himself referred to as Rudolph before, Terry asked Buddy Randolph why Pam and Dale would call him that. Randolph teased his friend and said it was because of his glowing nose and how Terry was always sticking it in others' business. Needless to say, Buddy Randolph's poor explanation of why Terry would be nicknamed Rudolph by Pam and Dale was not convincing. It was evident that Randolph possessed either the supernatural ability to hear conversations several miles away and through walls, or that he was psychic to a certain degree. Otherwise, how could he possibly have known about the nickname? Randolph clearly offered the potential existence of the nickname to his friend to see if Terry would confirm its existence by correcting Randolph about who Rudolph truly referred to.

Between his bag of tricks and supernatural powers, Buddy Randolph was a magician who ultimately caught the attention of interrogator Ian. During one of Ian's visits to Greene County, he had the pleasure of meeting Randolph for himself and, although no magic was performed that day, Ian did walk away with one of the magician's secrets. Ian allegedly spotted a tiny symbol of the number 13 tattooed on Randolph's hand. Perhaps 13 is Randolph's lucky number. Or perhaps the number 13 represents something quite different from luck to its branded owner. The number 13 is representative of many things. For instance, 13 is symbolic of The Last Supper, which depicts Jesus' last meal with his twelve disciples. Judas is counted as the 13th apostle, the man who betrayed Jesus. Additional Biblical symbology of the number 13 include the 13th Psalm, which reads, "The fool has said in his heart, There is no God," and the 13th chapter of Revelations is reserved to the Antichrist and the Beast. The 13th arcanum of the Tarot of Marseille corresponds to the tarot card "death." In both ancient and modern cultures around the world, 13 is considered positive and lucky, but to others superstition shrouds the number and is believed to be unlucky. Some hotels have no room number 13 and sometimes no 13th floor will be found in buildings with several stories. Let's not forget Friday the 13th! Some kabbalists view 13 as representing the snake, the dragon, the murderer and Satan. The number 13 is also the chosen symbol for the international gang MS-13 whose members can be found with a 13 tattooed in a highly visible place such as on the face, neck or hands.

Ian's discovery of Randolph's tattoo led me to wonder about MS-13. I wondered if a gang like that could be here in our town. During our research and snooping, my mom and I have come across dozens and dozens of questionable individuals, most of whom do have several tattoos, but none that ever really stood out. We found a couple Aryan Brotherhood gang members in this area, but no one that readily appeared to belong to MS-13. My mom and I might not have found anyone associated with major international criminal gangs, but we did find a slew of criminals, some of whom found a place on our player list. Now is the time to comb through those players, my sleuths.

There are many, and in a great effort to write about them in a somewhat cohesive manner, I will attempt to weave each of them into the story as best I can. The following face bubble masterpiece is my attempt at a flow chart, which is supposed to help illustrate how our players are or might be connected to Jessie in relation to how I'm going to unfold this portion of the story. Looking at the face bubble flow chart, you can see that this shit is complicated and, in spite of how I've organized it for story-telling purposes, all these people know each other. If the flow chart's purpose was to illustrate how these people are all connected, we would be staring at a tangled web, which is exactly what this is. Please keep in mind that not every player is considered a suspect (to me and my mom), some are just relevant to our story. Additionally, it is important to remember that all individuals are innocent until proven guilty and there is no proof whatsoever of any of the following players having anything to do with Jessie and her unborn baby's death. Refer to the player profiles in Chapter Three as needed. Welcome to seven degrees of Jessie Morrison.

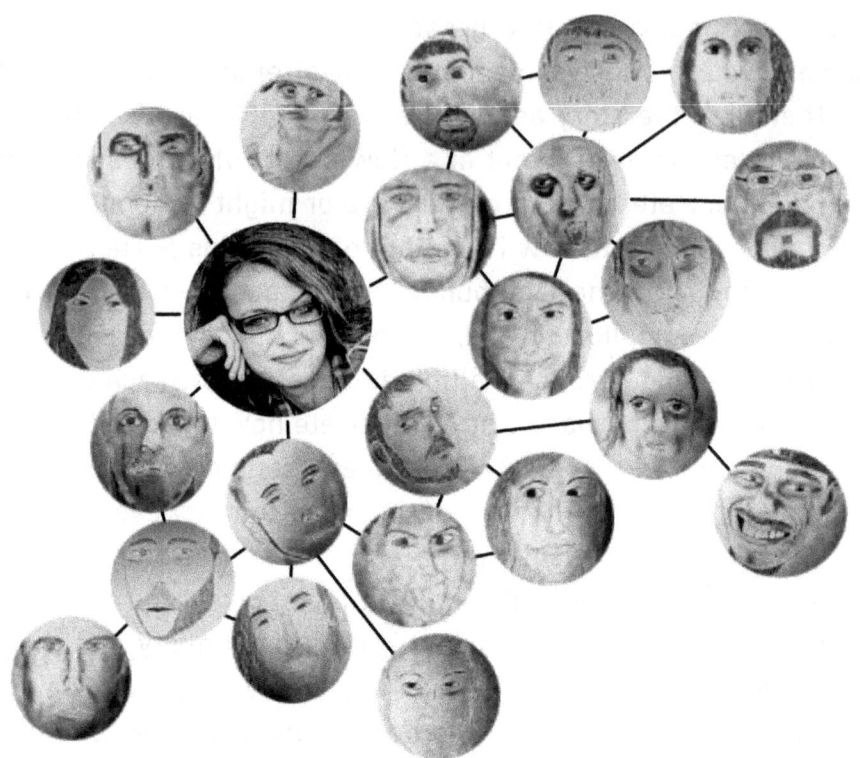

Jessie is featured in the "center" with the largest face bubble and directly connected to her are seven people I selected for varying reasons. Let's start with her mother, Susan, who is positioned to Jessie's left. Susan has claimed that she had plans with Jessie that day/night to spend time with her grandsons. When she couldn't get hold of Jessie and later found she wasn't at home, Susan began her search for her daughter. It's rumored, however, that Susan might have been less than two miles down the road from Jessie's place at an old friend's house located on Old Baileyton Road. Susan was allegedly at this friend's house around 5pm, was acting unusual, and by 6pm was talking about filing a missing person report for her daughter.

According to a news article about Susan's testimony, Susan left her home in Rogersville and drove 45 minutes to her daughter's house to see if Jessie was at home because she had allegedly not been answering her phone. Not finding her daughter at home, Susan then went to Vonda's house. Vonda has stated that Susan showed up at her home around 11pm. If Susan arrived at Vonda's at approximately 11pm and it takes roughly 8 minutes to drive from Jessie's house to Vonda's, this means Susan might have left her daughter's house around 10:50pm. We do not know how much time she spent at Jessie's when she first got there, but she presumably searched around the house and likely spent a few minutes talking to John. So we'll imagine she was at Jessie's for up to 20 minutes before driving over to Vonda's. We can estimate that Susan might have initially arrived at Jessie's on Cross Anchor around 10:30pm, which means she left her own home in Rogersville around 9:45pm.

If Susan truly did have plans to meet up with Jessie that day to visit with her grandsons and if her being at a friend's house between 5pm and 6pm on Old Baileyton Road is not true, then 9:45 at night is a reasonable hour to begin worrying about her daughter's whereabouts and for her to get in her car to find Jessie. Susan's actions that evening, whether they were propelled by a mother's fear of the unknown or a mother's secret knowledge of what had happened, suggest that Susan was concerned about Jessie. Can we say the same about Jessie's boyfriend/"fiancé"?

Moving counterclockwise from Susan, we wind our way to JT. JT and his friend, Bradley, who is positioned just below JT in the flow chart, were at the trailer on Cross Anchor Park that afternoon. JT testified that he and Bradley had stopped by his house for one reason or another and saw the groceries that Vonda and Jessie had bought. JT has said that he and Bradley were driving his son Benjamin's white van that day, so we can assume JT was the driver. Patrick, the neighbor who testified to witnessing Jessie get into a white van with two white males around 5:30pm, curiously only stated that Jessie got into a "white van." This is interesting to me because Patrick was their neighbor and must have been acquainted with Jessie, John and JT. With JT living there and being friends with Bradley, and sometimes Benjamin staying there as well, surely Patrick would have seen a white van there before. Had he never seen or been introduced to JT's youngest son and John's brother, Benjamin? Could he not recognize the van or who was in it? Perhaps Patrick's testimony was purposefully vague. I just think a neighbor might be able to divulge some more detail than what he did. Perhaps Patrick was reluctant to give any specifics. It is interesting that he moved away not long after Jessie's murder. Patrick also exhibited cold feet just prior to the trial. Vonda's defense attorney Steven required him as a witness. Patrick was to testify to speaking with Jessie that afternoon and to witnessing her leave in a white van, but Patrick allegedly never showed up and Steven allegedly sent an officer to fetch him. We know Patrick likely didn't lie about what he witnessed because half an hour later, the white van (or two white vans) appeared at Vonda's house. I wonder, did JT give Patrick some friendly advice on the content of his testimony? What if the white van that Jessie left in was already at the house when she got home? What if JT and Bradley were there at that time and saw the groceries, rather than having been there earlier as JT stated in his testimony? If that is true, then Jessie left in the white van with JT and Bradley, but then where the hell was Vonda's car? Was it left behind or was Patrick "confused" about what he had seen and Jessie got into Vonda's car to return it herself rather than getting into the van with the guys? Regardless of whether Jessie got into that damn van with JT or not, a DNA sample from Jessie's panties partially registered as JT's, so there's that.

Benjamin is located to the right of his father on the map. Benjamin was very close with Jessie. It would not be farfetched to say that they were best friends. If it is true that JT and Bradley were driving Benjamin's white van that day, where was Benjamin and where was Bradley's white van? Can we trust JT was telling the truth about which white van they were in? In his testimony, he claimed that he and Bradley saw the groceries Vonda and Jessie had bought and that they had been at the house around 3:45pm. But Jessie and Vonda didn't check out of Food City until 3:37pm and wouldn't have made it to Jessie's house until around 4pm. Did JT get confused about what time he and Bradley were at the trailer or did he lie on the stand? Perhaps the pair were in Bradley's white van after all and perhaps Benjamin's van was in his possession that day. We might not be aware of Benjamin's alibi for that evening, but he did post to his Facebook a few days after Jessie's death a smiling selfie, and on his cheek was a cut the size and shape of a fingernail. Note the date of 8/19/16 at the bottom left.

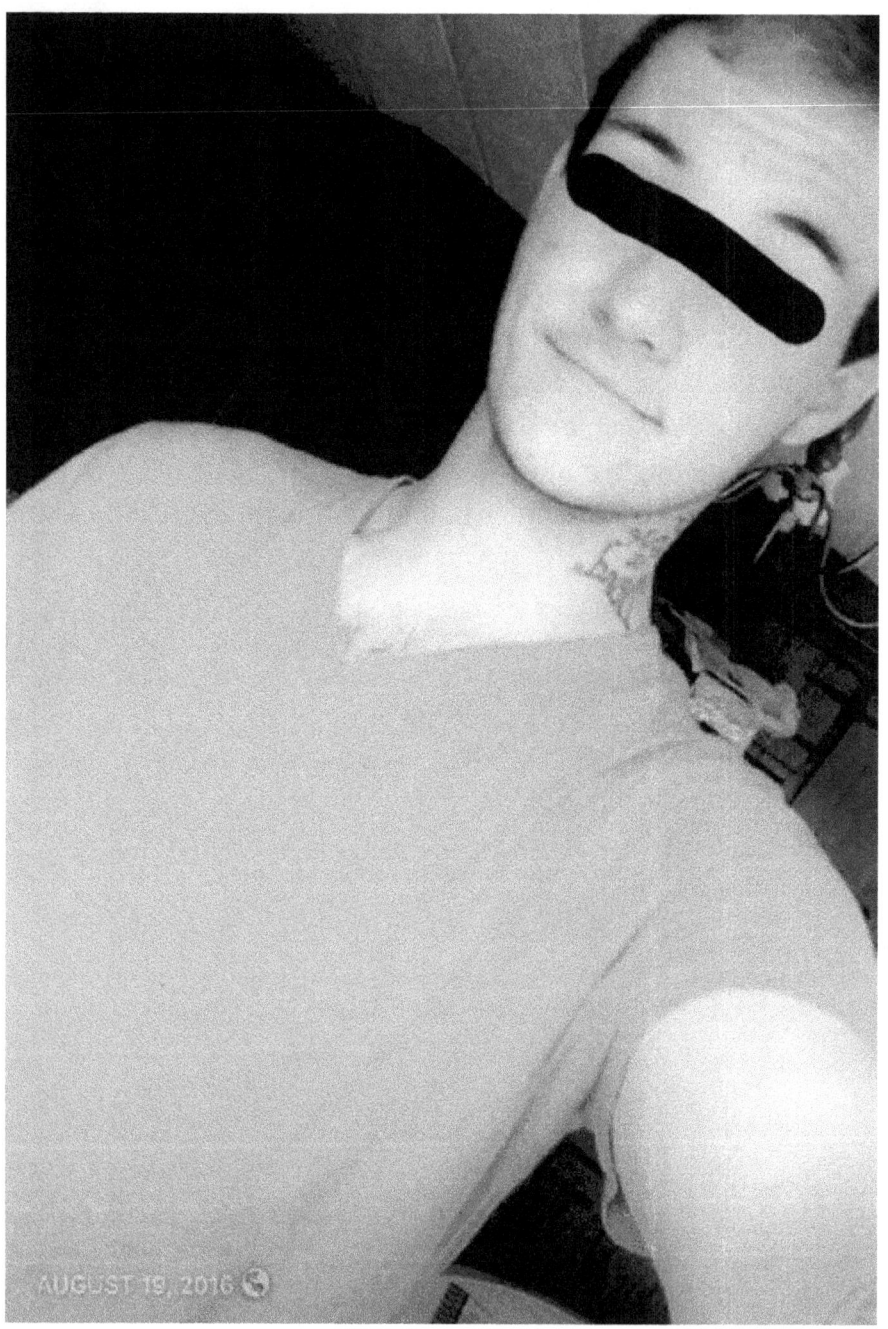

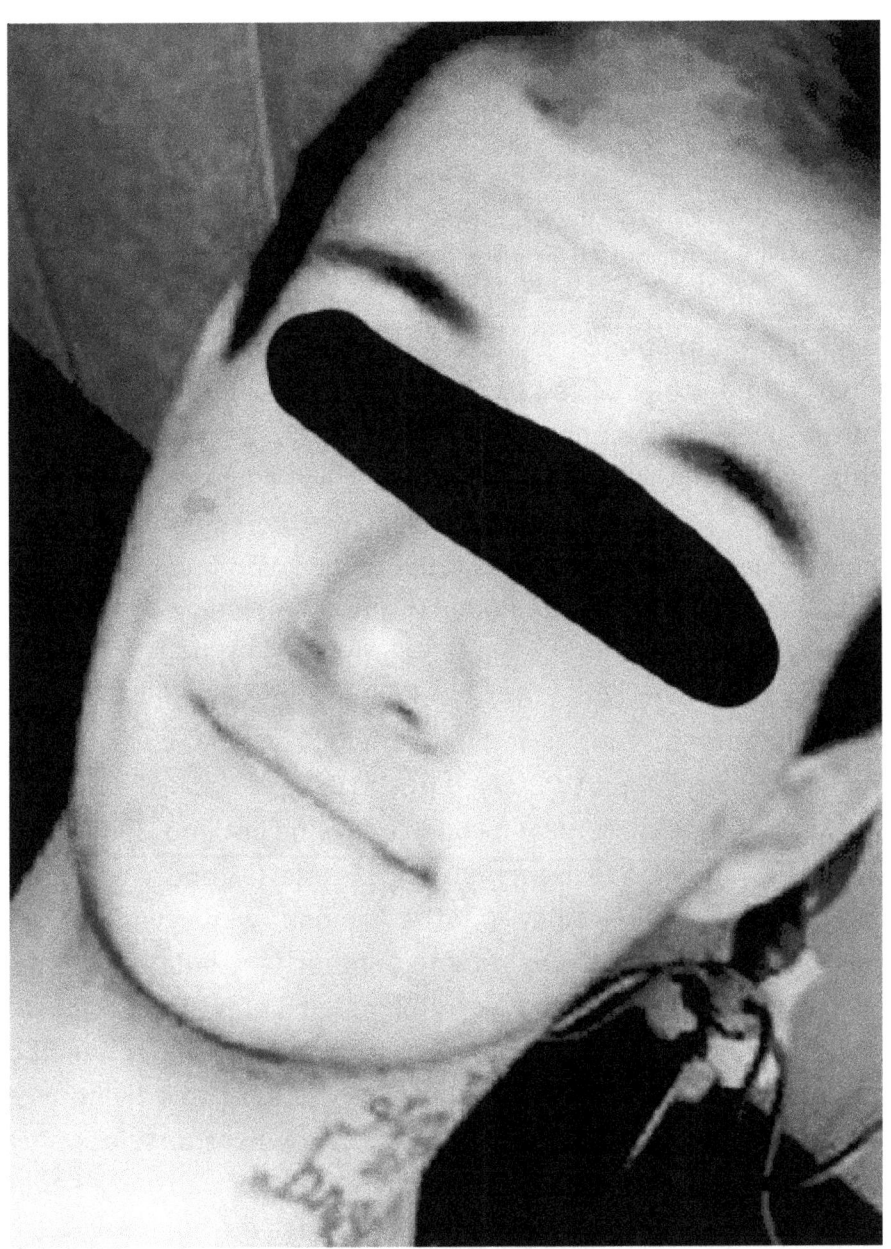

Benjamin also claimed, in a Facebook post, that he was so upset about what had happened to Jessie that he couldn't bring himself to attend her funeral. What kind of best friend and future uncle to your child doesn't attend your funeral? Whether he actually ended up attending or not, I do not know.

Patrick testified to seeing one white van at Jessie's house that evening but Vonda has stated that 30 minutes later, at approximately 6pm, she possibly saw two white vans down in the road near her driveway. What the crap?! I tell you what, if I never have to think about white vans for the rest of my life after this I will be more than happy. We might assume that the two white vans (if Vonda did indeed see two) belonged to Bradley and Benjamin. Perhaps Jessie did return Vonda's car herself because she knew Vonda had plans to go pick up Jemma later that evening. Perhaps the white van that was at Jessie's house followed her over to Vonda's, and when they arrived Benjamin met everyone at Vonda's in his own white van. Maybe it was a fucking white van party.

Perhaps Jessie returned Vonda's car and got into Benjamin's van with him. Maybe Benjamin and Jessie (in one white van) followed JT and Bradley (in the second white van) to go somewhere. Perhaps they went to another face bubble's house. The pretty dude with the scruff located below Benjamin on our flow chart is Travis. You can see that Travis is connected to both Benjamin and Bradley. Travis was allegedly living in a house on Jud Neal Loop not too far from where Jessie's body was eventually discovered. I covered this theory already, about how Jessie might have found herself at Travis' house with JT, Bradley and Benjamin, so I won't repeat that theory, but that is how those individuals are connected and might be relevant to how Jessie died.

The scary face bubble in the bottom left corner is Lee. Lee also lived on Jud Neal Loop, was Travis' neighbor, and was friends with Bradley at the time of Jessie's death. He's also the man responsible for blowing Alice's leg off with a shotgun, among other crimes, and is still awaiting trial, over two years later.

Now we've hit a dead-end on our flow chart, so let's retrace our steps back up to Benjamin. Connected to him is a hellcat named Miranda, who happens to look more like a drowned cat in her mugshot, but nevertheless is a badass with a criminal record to prove it. Miranda has made our player list for all kinds of intriguing reasons. I have not been able to confirm if she was friends with Jessie or even knew her, but Miranda is BFF with Benjamin these days. You'll have to refer to her player profile in Chapter Three for her details, but I will expand on a couple of her charges by way of a story. Once upon a time, Miranda was driving down the road at night and failed to dim her headlights to oncoming traffic. The oncoming vehicle she blinded was a cop. Said cop pulled a U-turn and attempted to pull her over. Well, our hellcat was not having that! Little girl put the pedal to the metal and a high-speed chase ensued. Whilst fleeing from the po-po at speeds reaching 100mph+, she proceeded to throw shit out of her vehicle at the cop in pursuit. Why is this story more than just entertaining? Because it illustrates that Miranda throws shit out of a vehicle while driving. If Jessie's personal belongings were in fact "thrown" out along Betsy Ross Road and Tyne Gray Road where they were later found by Detective Randolph, then Miranda might be a possible candidate for the job.

It gets better, sleuths, so crack another cold beer. At the time of Jessie's death, Miranda was living on Tyne Gray Road… the same road on which a few of Jessie's belongings were found and the same road her cell phone was later pinged on. Not only was Miranda living somewhere on Tyne Gray, she also has relatives that live on that same stretch of road. In fact, it could have been her relative's house that the cell phone pinged nearest to. There was unknown female DNA found on Jessie's body and there was also unknown female DNA found in Vonda's car. Could this DNA belong to Miranda? What motive could she have possibly had to kill Jessie? Miranda herself is a mother, would she have the balls (or heart) to murder a pregnant mother? Based on my light research of the topic, women typically commit homicide if they have something to gain. Out here, you can get killed over 300 bucks, or so I've been told. I should mention that getting killed over that amount of money is likely only to happen if you're involved in the drug scene, but Jessie did have $1,000 cash on her, and not only did she live with an alleged drug dealer, she was friends with both users and dealers.

The third face bubble connected to Benjamin is his mother, Linda. Oh, Linda. I don't doubt she didn't murder Jessie, but she has been known to be violent toward innocent things and her Mama Bear mode is fierce. Aside from her ever-entertaining and gloriously trashy Facebook posts, an intriguing exchange unfolded on her Facebook page recently. I now present to you Linda's rage against her son John's wife, Christy.

LINDA
3 hrs ·

Just for everyone to know CHRISTY and her little bitch ass sister talking shit on Facebook saying I broke into the house ripped up baby pictures stole TVs everything else is a lying cunt conniving little bitch this coming from someone who faked a pregnancy just to say she miscarried LOL what a joke and if it was it didn't belong to my son cuz the bitch was in and out of town she took my $500 and blew it stole the money my son left her to pay bills with it sounds like someone on drugs to me she to everything I ever owned in back of a truck with shit all over it nasty bitch they found the TVs that were stolen the landlord took them she cut her wrist just to say that it was done to her they found out she lied about that she was caught in a bar trying to ride up on a nasty hoe me looking motherfuker she is psychotic she's not supposed to be around the baby by herself they're saying she's so fucking crazy it's hard telling what she will do so you dumb little bitch stop with your threats stop with your harassment and trust me you will not supposed to be back at that trailer after you took some things and ran away with a baby not letting no one to know where you were at your dad's LOL you stupid hore and you are not even supposed to be in Tennessee you are supposed to be in Florida and that coming from the state after you OD'd on a bunch of pills you brought back from Florida with the baby in the house with you and let's pray you never try to lay hands on this this is a real fucking woman

LINDA
3 hrs · 🌐

Not to mention while she was having an ultrasound done I had my phone recording the whole time and it says on the recording the lady telling her I don't see nothing

LINDA
3 hrs · 🌐

Come on little girl ball is in your court now bitch I'm waiting to hear something from you you got me on the road you wanted to get some shit started bitch here I am mother fucker let's get it girlfriend get the fuck up be a real fucking woman get up in my face bitch

LINDA
3 hrs

She is a money-grubbing psychotic slasher has been cutting herself since she was 10 that sounds to me like someone who doesn't need to be with a baby by her self she even picked my sons step brother up had him to go out to the trailer to watch it until LINDA gets here she told him that she was going to Florida to be with my son it was all a fucking lie no one could find her she changed her number everything and she took the baby not letting his daddy know anything about where he was not shit you stupid crazy fucking bitch you're lucky you left Tennessee

OK, so to be fair, this is probably less Mama Bear mode and more psycho mode, but you get the picture. Christy's reply is as follows...

CHRISTY

Lol all I have to say is you seriously need to see a psychologist there is something wrong in your head. There's no question you ransacked stole and vandalised the house the neighbors seen you the cops seen you here and the landlord seen you here. Nobody else is going to rip pictures of me and my son throw out groceries to rot in the house write LINDA on the walls and all the other crazy shit that was done. As far as the things you said about me, I don't know how you come up with half of it. Drs don't just tell you you are having a miscarriage it's a medical diagnosis. As far as drugs, never have I. And as far as cheating on JOHN, i haven't. I just find it funny the only time u tell JOHN that is when I piss you off. What a mother you are. And nobody ever said I can't be alone with my son. That's just made up in your crazy head along with me driving all the way to Florida for pills. I truly feel sorry for you. You literally spent the past few days just rambling on about me on FB. I haven't talked to u in a week. And all of this started because you don't know how to respect people's households and try to bully people into doing what you say. All I can say is I'm not the one, it don't work on me. And just so you know, recording my ultrasound is against hospital policy and is a violation of HIPPA laws. And also all of this is slander. Along with all the threats u have made and mamaw made I'd be careful. And also JOHN knows what tools are missing. You were the only one who knew where JOHN hid his chainsaw and stole his beer also. He's not stupid. He knows you did it. And for the final time you don't have shit at this house. You got everything when u broke into my home while i was having my miscarriage. And here is the picture once again since u want to keep hollaring I was not pregnant. And   i don't really know what there is to like about this. Family or not you don't destroy someone's household because they make u mad. That is my sons home. This is YOUR SONS HOME **LINDA** . So again, what a great mom you are. Stealing and trashing not only your sons home, but the grandson you claim you are so worried about.

Sleuths, what you just read might be a window into both Linda and Christy's worlds. Linda's post highlights her readiness to fight, and if what Christy alleges about Linda in her reply is true, then Linda might very well be unstable. On the other hand, if what Linda alleges in her post is true, Christy might be unstable. This is the Tom foolery bullshit my mom and I try to wrap our brains around on any given day with this case. Feel free to make your own assumptions about the train wreck you just witnessed.

Linda might be ready to rumble, and she might have allegedly grossly neglected the cats and dogs once found dead in and outside of the home she shared with her son, Benjamin, but that doesn't make her a murderer of humans. Linda might not have Jessie's blood on her hands, but what she does have is family in law enforcement. It's unknown if she's John's birth mother or not and I say that only because my mom and I haven't been able to confirm that. The family trees out here are, at times, seemingly warped, and investigations of them sometimes yield confusing-ass results. For all intents and purposes, and for the purposes of this book, we will say that Linda is John's bio mother. And that being said, if Linda has a family member or two in law enforcement, then John does, too. Remember, out here, kin are kin and favors abound.

Moving right along in our flow chart, we'll go ahead and use Linda and Christy's little tiff as a segue over to Christy herself. There was the incident, of course, when John allegedly accidently fractured her skull that one time and the fact that she might allegedly be a bit cray-cray if you believe a word Linda has said about her, but as far as I know and based on what Christy has told me herself, she didn't even know Jessie. So Christy is not our bad guy, but she has proved relevant to this story and that is why she won a spot on the player list and her very own face bubble.

Rounding out, or should I say "cornering" out our little Bermuda Triangle of face bubbles we've found ourselves in, let's sail up to John. I'll preface our discussion about this dude by first telling you that my mom and I have added and removed him so many times from our special list of names that we are now cross-eyed and thoroughly confused. Freakin' John. What am I going to do with you? He had a solid alibi, but where was he after he got off work and what was he doing? Without being present at the trial myself and without having read the trial transcripts, I can only rely on what local newspapers reported about his testimony, which wasn't more than a fart in the wind. Like, was he worried about Jessie and her boys? He had to have been home from work approximately 3 hours before Susan showed up looking for Jessie. What was his exchange with Susan when she got there and why the hell did he not go with her to Vonda's? A local news article reported that after Susan left Vonda's house she went back to Jessie's to help John "search" for clues around the house or whatever. Did this guy just go to sleep after Susan left to file a missing person report at the police station? My mom and I can find NOTHING about John's reaction or actions that night. When shit is left to my imagination, it's generally not good.

Another red flag raised about him is Vonda's claim that John was allegedly one of the men who assaulted and threatened her that October night in 2016. Vonda alleges that John threatened to hurt Manning if she didn't stop snooping and if she didn't keep her mouth shut. In John's defense, after over a year of sleuthing, my mom and I both highly, highly doubt that he would ever harm a child. He just doesn't fit the profile. It appears John loves kids and they love him. He might not be the best father, but my guess is that if John ever did threaten to hurt a kid, it was likely an empty threat and only meant as a scare tactic.

Speaking of scare tactics, in all our sleuthing, my mom and I never really came across any malicious Facebook posts or comments from John. On the contrary, even when a scorned ex-girlfriend bashed him in a public Facebook post, he replied very calmly. The tiff between his mother Linda and his wife

Christy never drew a comment from him either, at least not on social media. We can never know what his character might be like behind closed doors, but from what my mom and I could find, John appears to be pretty damn passive. There are always two sides to every story and everything we hear and read about John is mostly contradictory, which is what makes it so difficult to definitively decide if he's a good guy or a bad guy. In the spirit of sleuthing, I'll leave the matter of John for you to mull over. Something to consider, however, is if John threatening a child sounds out of character for him, perhaps he was instructed to say what he allegedly said to Vonda and do what he allegedly did to her. Honestly, what could have been his motive for tracking Vonda down and allegedly assaulting her? Not to mention, how in the hell did he find her while she was driving home from the store? Does John share the same supernatural powers Detective Randolph seems to possess? Either John is also a magician or he's the magician's white rabbit, used for performing a trick.

Regardless of John's potential as somebunny's white rabbit (you see what I did there?), he might have skills when it comes to slight of hand tricks. In our face bubble chart, John is connected to women he has been in a relationship with, excluding his mother Linda (I hope). John is now married to Christy, whom we've discussed, and obviously dated Jessie, but to the immediate right of his rather evil-looking face bubble, we have Britney. I introduced Britney some time back and provided screen shots of Facebook posts she made, lamenting about how John is a shit father and blah blah blah. Well, just a week or two after Jessie's death, Britney seemed to have a change of heart regarding John. He apparently went to visit his son now that he was released from Jessie's allegedly controlling clutches and Britney couldn't have been happier about it. I don't have an incredible amount of dirt on this chick, and it's currently 2:00 in the morning right now as I write this and I'm tired as hell, so the point here is that Britney might possibly have had a motive to harm Jessie. Britney seemed pissed at Jessie for allegedly not allowing John to see his child and she might have even been jealous of Jessie because Jessie had her man. Playing pretend, if Britney allegedly murdered Jessie, she did have something to gain.

For you, dear reader, this is just the next paragraph, but for me it's a brand-new day because I finished the previous paragraph about Britney in the wee hours of the morning. Let's scoot on down to Brendon, who's connected to Britney and whose face bubble is hanging off the bottom right corner of her amusing mugshot. Judging by the scabs scattered across his face, he may or may not do meth. Judging by his arrest record, he does allegedly do meth. Take a pause here and flip back to Chapter Three and check out Brendon's player profile. You won't be disappointed. Brendon has a lengthy arrest record and a colorful one at that. I have no idea if he knew Jessie and I'm not certain when he started dating Britney, but the two of them have known each other for years and make a regular Bonnie and Clyde. Brendon is friends with the majority of players on our list, but I chose to connect him directly to Britney on the flow chart because they're in a relationship (at the time of this writing). Anyone with a criminal record and within a couple degrees of Jessie gets featured on the player list, within reason. Brendon might not have killed Jessie, but he does appear to be a bad dude. He's also friends with one of our players by the name of C.R., who lived on Cross Anchor the same time Jessie was living there.

Now we need to retrace our steps and find our way back to John on the flow chart. The girl connected to him at the top right corner of his bubble is Nicole. Nicole once dated John and in a Facebook post about him allegedly fracturing Christy's skull, she seemed to be happy about John's "true" character having been revealed. Nicole once told a friend of mine that while she was in a relationship with John he was allegedly secretly dating both Britney and Jessie as well. Over time, he eventually left Nicole for the other girls and then ultimately left Britney for Jessie. Nicole is friends with Black Eyes, whose face bubble is just above her own, and the pair may or may not have gotten into some trouble with the law early in 2019. I have no reason to believe Nicole had anything to do with Jessie's death, but nothing would surprise me these days. She made the list because she's friends with many of the players on our list and is a person the producers have taken an interest in. Although the producers cannot share any information with me about their investigation, I believe Nicole is sharing information with them.

Nicole once dated Damien, the creep to the right of her face bubble. Damien is another one who's friends with most of the players on our list. Again, I don't know if he was friends with Jessie or ever met her, but he dated Nicole for quite some time. In my wildest imagination, Nicole could have been allegedly jealous of Jessie or still pissed off at John or both, and sometimes scorned ex-girlfriends enlist the help of their current beaus for revenge. This might not be the case with Nicole and Damien, but anything is possible.

Nicole and Damien are connected to Black Eyes, creating another intriguing Bermuda Triangle. Black Eyes is easy to locate on the flow chart because she has two fat shiners, which she acquired sometime in December 2018. Black Eyes, honestly, could be at the center of the flow chart surrounded by all our players because she's friends with all of them but maybe two. Black Eyes has had her fair share of run-ins with the law and is allegedly no stranger to the drug scene. I assume she must also be of some importance because the producers seem to have a special interest in her too. The producers' interest in Black Eyes likely means she has information to share and, although she doesn't strike me as a killer, she's relevant to this story because she's friends with so many "bad guys." Also, both Jessie and Black Eyes dated Vonda's son, Wyatt.

Black Eyes' special connection to Wyatt and her being his most recent girlfriend might be a reason she's found favor with the producers. Wyatt's face bubble is located at the top right corner of Jessie, in between her other two baby-daddies, John (presumably the father of her unborn baby) and Shane, the father of her youngest son Sam. Wyatt and Jessie met through her mother, Susan. A few years ago, Susan and Wyatt were alleged "associates." Wyatt has told me that Susan was the one that introduced him to Jessie. Wyatt was 28 years old when he first got together with Jessie, who was approximately 17 years old and underage. You tell me how a mother in her right mind is going to let a 28-year-old man have anything to do with her 17-year-old daughter and then we'll both know. What the hell kind of parenting is that? In my mind, Susan allowing that to occur is not much different than pimping her daughter out. Jessie became pregnant with Manning sometime in May 2012 and might not have even completed her junior year in high school yet. She would have started her senior year three months pregnant and given birth fourth months before graduating.

Wyatt was never really part of his son Manning's life at first. However, after Vonda had entered Jessie and Manning's lives, Wyatt did make somewhat of an effort. He might not have been an involved father, but he really had no motive to kill Jessie. Not to mention, Wyatt had an alibi the night Jessie was murdered, was cleared by the county and has fully cooperated with Ian and the producers, giving them tons of information, which has left him looking over his shoulder. Ian's audio recording of Vonda allegedly suggesting and/or outright saying that it was Wyatt she saw return her car that night could be damning for Wyatt if the audio recording is genuine and unaltered. Wyatt's alibi places him in Limestone that night at a house party, but he didn't arrive there until sometime after 6:30pm.

Wyatt's girlfriend at the time, Janet, has stated that they shared a single car and that she took the car to work that day, leaving Wyatt at the house. She's told me that she got home from work at approximately 6:30pm, and when she walked in the door Wyatt was already showered, dressed and ready to head over to Limestone with her. Wyatt claims he can't remember what he did that day and doesn't remember leaving the house. Without a witness to put Wyatt at the house that day, or even just that afternoon, we'll have to play detective.

Janet says she got home from work at approximately 6:30pm. From the house she and Wyatt were living in at the time, it takes approximately 18 minutes to the location where Jessie's body was found. If Wyatt was already showered and dressed by 6:30pm, then the latest he could have gotten back home, if he ever did leave, would have been 6:15pm, giving him 15 minutes to shower and dress for the house party. If he did leave and did arrive back home at 6:15pm, and pretending he murdered Jessie, he would have been at the location on Jud Neal Loop disposing of her body at approximately 5:55pm. Vonda's car was returned to her around 6:00pm and she lives roughly five minutes from the location where Jessie's body was found. With this theory, the times seem to be perfect, but the notion that Wyatt participated in Jessie's murder hinges very carefully on exact times, which we do not have. However, it does appear that it could have been possible for Wyatt to have killed her if she was killed prior to 5:55pm. This is one of those moments where an estimated time of death would come in handy, but someone didn't do their damn job. In spite of it being possible that Wyatt could have killed Jessie, his DNA was not found on Jessie or at the crime scene.

Next, Cody is the guy connected to Wyatt on the flow chart. He's the one that started work with the same employer and on the same day as Wyatt. Just a day or so after their first day on the job, Cody was all up in Wyatt's shit. Mind you, Wyatt didn't know Cody from Adam. Wyatt told me that Cody was asking questions about Vonda and offered Wyatt money to drive him down to Atlanta. Evidently this guy gushed his life story to Wyatt and freely told him that he was allegedly a plug for a cartel. Wyatt saw the red flags immediately and smelled a rat. When Wyatt told me about Cody, we both assumed he had been planted there because of Wyatt, but we couldn't figure out why. Now that Wyatt and I are no longer speaking, any updates about Cody have stopped, but I did find him on Facebook and saw that he's friends with many players on our list and other "bad guys." His girlfriend, Chasity, who got swept up with JT in that major drug bust in October 2018, also made a spot on our player list, but didn't seem relevant enough to include in the flow chart. Chasity, however, is close friends with Black Eyes. I imagine Cody did not murder Jessie, if he even knew her, but his claim of being a plug for a cartel and his tattoo of presumably a Latin Kings' five-point crown is very interesting and, since this case obviously has something to do with drugs, he wins a face bubble.

To the right of our Latin King is Litt. Dude deserves a face bubble because he's BFF with Dawn and because of drugs. I haven't discovered a motive he would have had to kill Jessie, but his friendship with Dawn and his friendships with a majority of the other players is relevant enough for me. The drug scene here is vast and he could have easily crossed paths that day with Jessie. There were three sets of unknown male DNA under Jessie's fingernails and there was one unknown male DNA sample in her panties, so any male criminal within a couple of degrees of Jessie is on my radar.

Litt's buddy, Dawn, can be found to the right of his face bubble. Oh, girl. Check out her player profile in Chapter Three. Dawn has a lengthy arrest record with varying charges and she's friends with some seedy people. I was told she allegedly lived near Vonda on Davis Valley Road at the time of Jessie's murder. I was also told that this woman allegedly started freaking out one night not long after Jessie was killed. I don't know the details or what she might have said, all I was told was that

Dawn was trippin' and appeared to be very worried about the circumstances surrounding Jessie's death. Obviously, Dawn's alleged behavior raises an eyebrow and leaves one wondering if she knows something or was possibly involved.

As with most players on our list, a man by the name of C.R. is friends with Black Eyes and is connected to her face bubble off to the far right. C.R. is "self-employed" and lived in the same tiny trailer park Jessie lived in. C.R.'s friends list on Facebook reveals a crowd of much younger females. The man knows many of the players on this list, and quite frankly, there's just something about his face that I don't like. He won a spot in the flow chart because he fits the profile. It's my personal opinion that he's involved in the drug scene and that's good enough for me.

C.R. rounded out the right side of the flow chart and all we're left with are Shane and Adam. Shane is the thug with a bandana covering his face, located above Jessie. Shane's airtight alibi was that he was in Texas at the time of Jessie's death, but that doesn't mean he doesn't have friends in low places to handle shit. In fact, he's friends with plenty of questionable people. Shane is Sam's father and, from what I understand, Jessie wouldn't let Shane see his son. Jessie wouldn't let Shane's mother, Amy, see her grandson either. Amy doesn't necessarily seem too interested in Sam anyway because if she was Susan wouldn't be raising him. Amy has friends across the spectrum, both in high places and low places. Shane might not have killed Jessie, but dude seems smug as fuck, so he wins a face bubble.

Last, but not least, is Adam. He's located in the top left corner. Adam and his parents are (or were) close friends with Susan. I was told that he and Jessie used to mess around, but never dated. It was at his parents' house where Susan allegedly found herself between 5pm and 6pm on the night Jessie was killed. Was Adam living at his parents' house just two miles down the road from where Jessie lived at the time? Did Adam have a jealous streak or maybe want to seek revenge if Jessie denied him? These are questions we don't have answers to, but he made the list because he and his family were long-time friends with Susan and Jessie. In fact, Vonda has told me that Adam's mother was allegedly going to come forward publicly with some information, but that she backed out when the moment came. I've also heard rumors that her husband has warned her to keep her mouth shut.

These are our players, my sleuths. Perhaps one or two of them killed Jessie and her unborn baby. Perhaps a few of them know what happened to her. It's difficult to decide whether Jessie's death was premeditated or not or if Vonda taking the fall for it was the plan all along. But one thing is for certain, Vonda has been wrongly convicted. Our pages here have dwindled down to this end, which is no end at all unfortunately. My investigation is ongoing, and my mom and I are hot on the trail of a brand-new lead and a very dangerous theory. We must prepare ourselves. The stakes are high and there is much to lose. The killer is still out there, and I hope he's sleeping with one eye open. I know that I've been. I will have more to tell, but I won't say a word until I'm no longer looking over my shoulder. Good-bye, devil's playground.

Wait for it...

Oh, sleuths... just as I submitted this completed manuscript to my publisher, something astounding happened to me and thus I've found myself in a position that warrants me sharing this turn of events with you now.

I hadn't received an e-mail from Vonda in several weeks and was waiting for her to reply to the last e-mail I sent her before I told her about this book I've written and the fortunate news of having found a publisher so quickly. Wyatt apparently let the cat out of the bag before I could tell Vonda myself because this was the e-mail Vonda sent me:

Inbox

Delete **Reply**

◀ Prev

Next ▶

From:
Date: 8/12/2019 7:20:56 PM
To: VONDA SMITH

Attachments: **NOVA WEST**

Ya, I'm fine. Heard you been doing alot. NOVA let me start out by saying. I didnt know in any way that the hours you and your mother spent in trying to help me you expected to get money . Nor did I think you would be writting a book. I thought it was because of LOVE. Boy was I wrong. I could have gotten that from HAILEY not you. Oh if I'm wrong please explain. Just know that, I have never agreed or authorized for anything I have said to you or anyone to be in a book or movie. I can't believe you, You honestly think you deserve money from Jessies death. Any money whatso ever should be put in trust fund for MANNING and SAM and then rest go to DON . Had I known that talking to you had a price I would have never !!!!!. Guess I'll see when your book comes out.

Vonda's e-mail to me reads as follows:

"Ya, I'm fine. Heard you been doing a lot. [Nova] let me start out by saying. I did'nt know in any way that the hours you and your mother spent in trying to help me you expected to get money. Nor did I think you would be writing a book. I thought it was because of LOVE. Boy was I wrong. I could have gotten that from [Hailey] not you. Oh if I'm wrong please explain. Just know that, I have never agreed or authorized for anything I have said to you or anyone to be in a book or movie. I can't believe you, You honestly think you deserve money from Jessies death. Any money whatso ever should be put in trust fund for [Manning] and [Sam] and then rest go to [Don]. Had I known that talking to you had a price I would have never!!!!!. Guess I'll see when your book comes out."

My initial reply to Vonda's e-mail was this:

✉ Sent

[Delete]

From:
Date:
Sent To:

NOVA WEST
8/12/2019 8:25:33 PM
VONDA SMITH

Attachments:

Ouch. Wow... I'm not sure who painted this picture for you of what's happening with the book, but they told you all wrong. I did write a book and I wrote the book with the intention of further helping your case, Von. It's not about the money... what the heck is wrong with you people and money?! I'm trying to HELP YOU because of LOVE! I'm trying to help Jessie have justice by finding her killer(s). My mom and I don't want any money... we've been working our butts off for justice, Von. I can't believe you actually think I would be such a crap person. More to the point... who ever said I wouldn't help **DON** financially? With you and WYATT attacking me over something ya'll don't have the details about makes ya'll look ignorant and greedy. Of course I will help **DON** if I'm able to! So the question is... if you think I'm only in this for the money, why are ya'll the ones with your hands out? That would be like me lining up with my hand out to you asking for money when you get out and sue the county. It wouldn't be right for me to ask you that. Shame on ya'll for jumping to conclusions... wow. At least now I know what I mean to "family". Ya'll got a funny way of asking for help. "You owe us the money you MIGHT make" isn't polite and it makes me feel like a worthless piece of crap... so much for that "love" you mentioned.

PS... if you want to be buddies with **HAILEY**, you be my guest... your attorney sure is.

The postscript was my way of letting Vonda know that my rival and her critic/enemy is Facebook friends with her attorney, which my mom and I recently discovered. Upon our discovery, I texted Vonda's son, Curtis, to let him know. His response was this:

CURTIS

—— 3 weeks ago ——

CURTIS, it's NOVA. My mom just discovered that STEVEN is Facebook friends with HAILEY! Wth?!

Aug 5 3:07 PM

So

Aug 5 3:09 PM

HAILEY has trash talked your mom and your family and me. Don't you find it odd that she's FB friends with your mom's attorney?

Aug 5 3:14 PM

His reply:

> No we don't care bout that shit. STEVEN has done everything mom has told him. I don't care who he has as a friend. We don't know anything about the situation and I'm not going to waste time on speculations. We are going with STEVEN to the end
>
> Aug 5 5:16 PM

Now, I don't know how you want to interpret Curtis' response, but I interpreted it as him being a dick. Although I support the faith one has in their attorney, I am suspicious as to why Steven would be Facebook friends with Hailey, a woman who has crusaded against my support for and defense of Vonda. I am also suspicious of Curtis' relationship with and absolute trust in Steven, when there have been certain instances and red flags that Curtis should have questioned but did not. He's always been so hell bent on trusting and defending Steven and there's just something about it that feels weird to me. I also find Curtis' comment about Steven doing everything Vonda has told him to do very, very curious. What exactly has Vonda told her attorney to do and not to do? Based on my latest experience with Vonda, which you just read about, and what Curtis has said about her obvious control over her attorney… it raises the question, who the hell does Vonda think she is? Her true colors have just come shining through, haven't they?

I'm getting the impression that she's a woman who wants to control everyone and everything, even from behind prison bars! I would venture to guess that Vonda can be very manipulative and I'm feeling incredibly uncomfortable about publishing this book now.

As a matter of fact, I took to Tumblr after receiving Vonda's e-mail:

Last Post

Dear sleuths... this is my final post. I have been confronted with something heartbreaking and astonishing.

Vonda and her son are very upset about the book I've been writing about the case. Their anger arises from arrogant entitlement. I have been chastised by each of them over the book deal and you won't believe why.

They want my money. They want the hypothetical, future money from the book that is not yet finished. They feel that they deserve any and all profits I might make from book sales.

Amusingly, they made their angry demands before I could tell them about the book myself... before I ever had the opportunity to share with them my plans for the money from the book.

Of course I would help them... just as I've been doing for the last 15 months of my life. I found a retired FBI agent to help with Vonda's case and a forensic specialist as well. I presented her case to director and producer, Joe Berlinger, whose team has been investigating the case and filming for a documentary.

I have maintained this blog for over a year now and I have fought for and defended Vonda and her son and I have risked a great deal and to thank me... they hatefully come to me with their hands out while scolding me about my "greed"... the same greed they're... being... greedy... about. Slow clap, everyone.

Writing a book about this case was always, only about another possible route to justice for Vonda and Jessie. Authors don't typically write for the money, we write because it's in our bones and part of our soul... and because we love it.

In light of this new bullshit, I made a difficult call to my publisher and told him the book cannot be published. He graciously allowed me to break my contract under the circumstances.

My decision to not publish is not because of Vonda's feelings or her own greed, but because I've simply had enough. I will not publish the book, I will no longer maintain this blog and I sure as hell am done with this case.

I feel defeated in every sense of the word and mostly... I'm just sad. I'm exhausted and confused and I greatly regret having ever gotten involved to begin with.

I'm hanging my hat, sleuths. I'm done and I'm getting the hell out of here.

Thank you for being a great audience. I'm sorry it had to end this way.

Goodbye.

After my final post on Tumblr, announcing to "the world" that I would no longer be publishing the book, I e-mailed Vonda a second time and that e-mail was much bolder. Three days had passed since I received her first e-mail and sent my initial reply, and in that time my emotional state had shifted from absolute shock and feeling wounded to anger. I adjusted my spine, put my big girl panties on, and fired back.

Date: 8/15/2019 1:33:53 AM

Sent To: VONDA SMITH

Attachments:

This is my second email to you in response to the hateful one you sent me on Jessie and her unborn baby's D-day anniversary, so if you haven't read that one first, I recommend you do so now.

I planned to wait for your response to my prior email, but I have some things I want to say and there seems to be no reason at all to wait to say them. After all, I'm not interested in participating in a song and dance routine by going back and forth with you about this. So I'll just say what I need to say and be done.

I posted my final post to my Tumblr blog last night. I told the world about your email to me and WYATT's texts. When I told you that I'm fighting for justice and the truth... you and your son are not exempt from that. I have publicly rained down on multiple people for their actions and now I've rained down on yours. You really should have approached me in a kinder manner.

Your foot-in-mouth disease has cost you not only your freedom, but has now also cost you any money I might have earned from the book on your behalf. See... you and WYATT never gave me the chance to offer anything because you both jumped to conclusions and attacked me before I could tell you that my publisher and I wanted to offer you a certain percentage of the net sales of the book... for life. In other words, you screwed yourself big time... which seems to be your best talent, seeing as how you're serving life behind bars for being dumb as shit. Allow me to illustrate your ignorance...

You chastised me for writing a book about this case (WHICH I WROTE IN DEFENSE OF YOU

AND YOUR LOSER SON) and then in the next sentence, you were telling me what to do with the money from the same book you're upset about me writing.

You suggested I give all my hypothetical money to your grandson, whom I've never met, yet... what has your own son done for him? Is WYATT sending his son money? Why in the hell should I flip the bill for some kid when his own dead beat father won't? You have lost your damn mind, Vonda.

Additionally, if you feel so strongly about a person "making a profit" by writing a book about a murder and that it's so wrong to do... then might I suggest you throw your Bible away and renounce Christianity. Jesus was murdered and the book written about him and his death has sold BILLIONS of copies for millenia.

You have audacity to point your finger at me from where you're sitting. I have done nothing but help you and your family through this mess that you created and you think you're in a high and mighty position to speak to me the way you did? Think again.

The book is no longer being published. I called my publisher and pulled the plug on it. You don't deserve anything more than the cell you're going to rot it. There will be no more of your story that I defend or fight for and there will be no money to help you or your family.

PS: You're a convicted felon... you have no rights. Anyone, anywhere, any time is free to write about you and this case... they don't need your permission. I was wanting to write a book about it first so that the true story would be out there, rather than a book full of half-truths... but you railroaded that, didn't you? The next author that comes along will probably not be so kind.

Just in case you missed it, this is our last communication. You betrayed me and I don't give second chances. If I wasn't so hurt and pissed at you, I would belly laugh at your utter ignorance. You seem to keep your mouth shut when you shouldn't and you spew shit when you should keep your trap shut. These are life lessons, of course and it's apparent you learn them the hard way.

Best of luck with the hard way...

BAZINGA! Yeah, it was a ruthless email to send, but… fuck it. In a strategic move, after all that has happened, I told my first lie to my Tumblr followers, and I spread that same lie to my family and Vonda. By announcing I was no longer publishing this book, I empowered many things. For starters, I proved to my audience that I'm not biased based on my final post about Vonda. Secondly, our fallout made for a clear ending to my posting on Tumblr. Most importantly, everyone is now under the impression that the book is not being published, which is the lie. I lied to protect myself and my kids and to buy us time to relocate. If everyone believes there's no book and no money, then they should leave me alone long enough for me to get my ducks in a row and get outta here.

The downside to posting what I did to Tumblr is Vonda and her sons, Wyatt and Curtis, reacting with vengeance. At this point, there would be no reason for them not to greenlight me or black spot me or put a hit out on me… or whatever the hell it is that shitty people do to get others harmed or killed. No one knows my pen name or the name of my publisher, and no one knows the title of the book. It's reasonable to think I could be safe… if it weren't for the woman I was trying to rescue.

Vonda knows my true identity and so do Wyatt and Curtis. Can I trust them to keep my anonymity after I blasted the truth on Tumblr? I took a huge risk in doing that and I'm hoping it pays off, but what will the repercussions be?

The swiftest repercussions came from a source with an unlikely stance. My rival blogger Hailey must be following my Tumblr blog because less than 12 hours after my final post she messaged my friend and relative of Vonda's. Hailey wanted to know if my "accusations" about Vonda and Wyatt were true. She wanted confirmation that they were ungrateful little shits who threw me (their rescuer) under the bus. Even she was astounded to learn that Vonda would behave this way toward the one person attempting to clear her name and free her from a wrongful conviction. Hailey did ultimately defend me to my friend. When even your enemy sides with you about what is right and what is wrong, you know someone fucked up.

Meanwhile, I'm over here texting my poor publisher all this shit that's unfolding and not only was he gracious enough to offer me an "out" (to break the contract), he insisted I offer Vonda a certain percentage of the book sales. As sweet and innocent a gesture as it was, I declined. Any money I might earn from the book sales will now be directed to my relocation fund and my lawsuit fund and my friggin' alcohol fund. Vonda thinks the money should go to her grandson? Pff… what has her own son provided him? Wyatt is Manning's freaking father! I'm not flipping the bill for a kid I've never met, especially when Vonda's own son won't step up to the plate and be a father. Like, are you fucking kidding me with this shit? How arrogant are you to point your finger at me when your loser son can't even take responsibility?! One thing is for damn sure… there will never be another instance of a convicted felon shaking their finger at me from a lifetime behind bars or I'll break it the fuck off.

Now, I'll let my lie about Devil's Playground not being published spread and see what happens. I would say at this point if anything ever happens to me, it's a possibility that Vonda and/or her family have a motive. Shit, I gave everyone in this book a motive to want to hurt me, but her immediate family are the only ones who know my identity (and where I live), and I wonder if they'll one day make a deal with the devil.

 **Inbox**

From: VONDA SMITH
Date: 8/17/2019 5:45:00 PM
To: NOVA WEST

Attachments:

You go Judas throw those stones.

I've always preferred to be transparent with people and to tell the truth and nothing but the truth (except for my recent lie about this book not being published, which only exists because of the flack I got when I initially told everyone the truth, that I was writing the book in the first place). They say the truth will set you free, but they also say that ignorance is bliss and that no good deed goes unpunished. I'm here to tell you that all three idioms are true. What I've learned from life, you must stand up for yourself and you absolutely should be standing up for others. Ironically, in my situation, the person I've been standing up for was the one to turn on me, which was unexpected, but that's life too.

    I don't know what will happen from here, but I have an uneasy feeling about it all. I've found myself in an awkward position, and this book, this thing that I created out of passion for something, was an accomplishment for me to write and I was proud and hopeful. Now any pride is gone and my passion for fighting the good fight has been shattered. How am I to go forward presenting and promoting the thing I've created when all I want to do is destroy it and try to leave it all behind me?

Sleuths, let me know what you think about the book, the case, the whole damn mess of it. Hopefully by the time you're reading this I've found my way out of the funk I now find myself in. Happier days and all that, right?

Much love,

Nova West

11/02/2019

P.S.

They say dead men tell no tales, but their obituaries sure can. I've just learned that John's uncle (his father's brother) recently and unexpectedly passed away. The man's obituary lists John as his son and John's child as his grandson. Further down in his obituary, John's siblings are listed as the man's niece and nephew. Until this moment, I was under the impression (as were the jurors) that JT was John's father. But if JT's brother (the man who passed away) is truly John's biological father and not in fact his "uncle," then Houston, we have a problem. On the other hand, it's more of a miracle. You see, during Vonda's trial, the prosecution presented JT to the courtroom as John's father. JT never corrected the prosecution or the defense and neither did John. If John is not JT's biological son after all, I would imagine that very fact alone could free Vonda. I'm no attorney, but could this be grounds for a mistrial or something? Let's not forget about the DNA found in Jessie's panties that initially registered as JT's but was determined to more than likely have been John's, due to the fact that father and son share such similar DNA. If JT is John's freaking uncle and not his father, then does that mean that the DNA that registered as JT's is definitively JT's? If it is his DNA, does that mean he could have raped Jessie? If he did, did he then kill her, too?

I emailed the producers this alarming discovery, whose Wrong Man Season Two trailer just dropped a couple of weeks ago. Season Two and Vonda Smith's episode will air beginning February 9, 2020 on the Starz network.

From our "desks" to yours, my mom and I thank you, sleuths. Stay tuned…

Facebook group: "Devil's Playground—A True Crime Story"

Twitter: @NovaWest_Author

Email: novawestauthor@gmail.com

www.ingramcontent.com/pod-product-compliance
Lightning Source LLC
Chambersburg PA
CBHW070042040426
42333CB00041B/1926